Objects of Affection

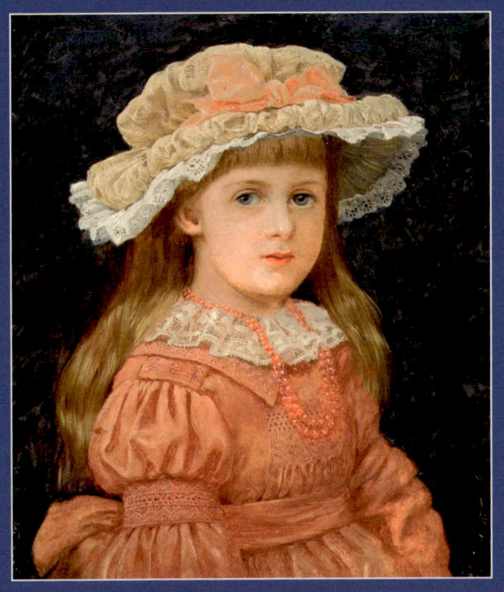

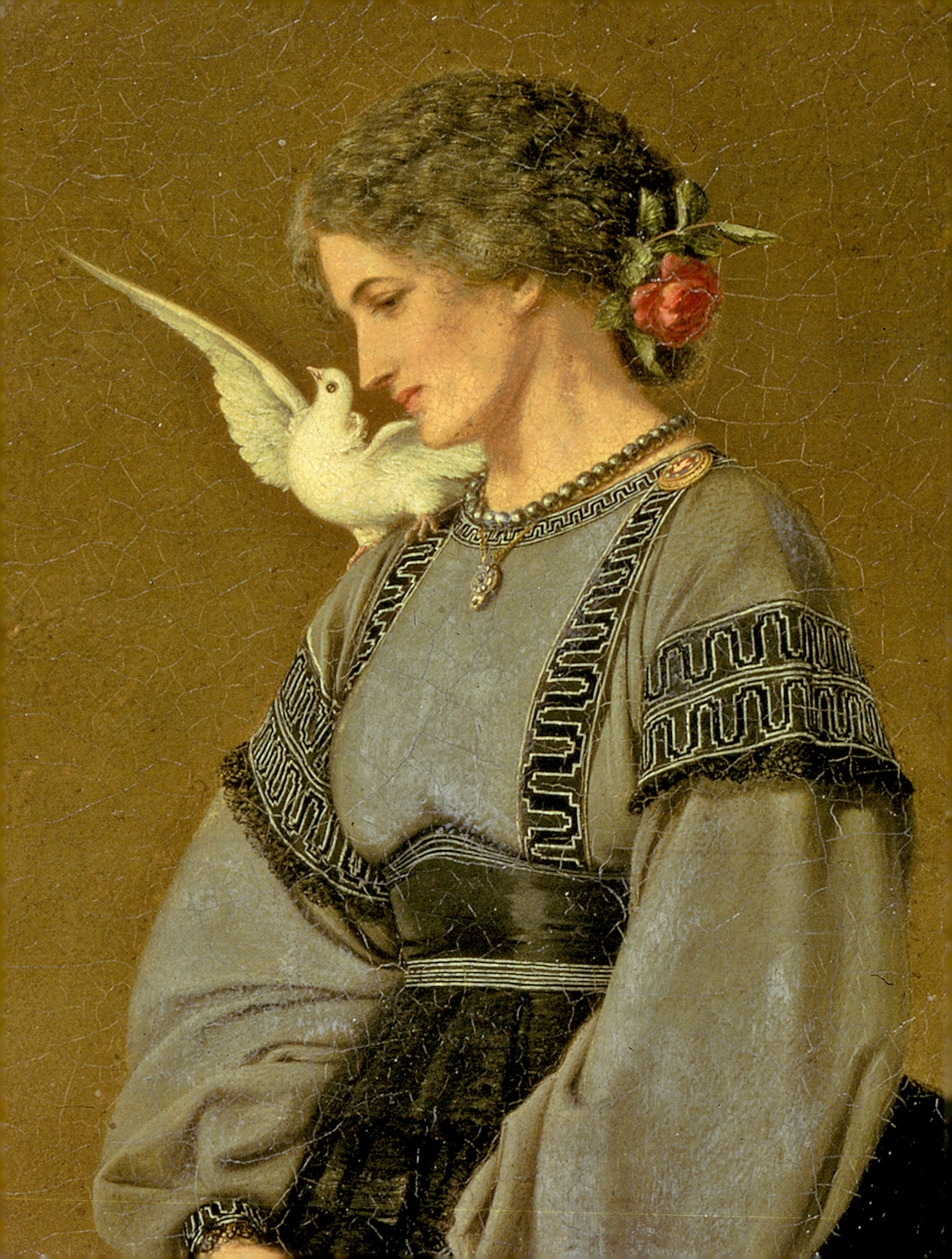

Objects of Affection

PRE-RAPHAELITE PORTRAITS BY JOHN BRETT

CHRISTIANA PAYNE

ANN SUMNER

Contents

Director's Foreword

The last ten years have seen a major evaluation of the career of the Victorian artist John Brett with exhibitions in Cardiff (2001) and Penzance (2006) and the publication this year of Christiana Payne's full assessment of his landscape paintings. This exhibition sheds new light on a little-known aspect of his work, his charming, individual and often very personal portraits, many of which are exhibited for the first time. They reveal much about Brett, his early career, friendships and attachments, as well as his pride in his growing family. It also highlights his extensive connections with Birmingham.

It was a privilege to curate the exhibition *John Brett: A Pre-Raphaelite on the Shores of Wales* at the National Museum of Wales in 2001 and encounter for the first time a group of Brett enthusiasts, including Charles Brett, who has done so much research on his great-grandfather, Christopher Gridley, and, of course, Christiana Payne. Charles and Christopher agreed to join our Exhibition Committee and have given Christiana and myself enormous support and encouragement over the past three years. I would like to pay particular tribute to them both. Two other colleagues on the Committee have also supported us tirelessly - Paul Spencer-Longhurst who first presented the exhibition proposal in 2007 on Christiana's behalf and Greg Smith who edited the catalogue and the interpretation for the show. The Brett family have provided much new information, especially Martin Brett, and once again many descendants have generously lent works, as well as contributing archival material. Other lenders, including Andrew and Christina Brownsword and Lord Margadale, have shared our enthusiasm for Brett and given us encouragement.

It has been a particular pleasure to work with Christiana Payne of Oxford Brookes University. She has been an understanding and sympathetic colleague as we worked on the catalogue, exhibition and the tour. We are indebted to the Paul Mellon Centre for Studies in British Art for their contribution to the catalogue production and to the Trustees of the Henry Barber Trust who support our exhibition programme. We also gratefully acknowledge the funding we receive from the Higher Education Funding Council for England (HEFCE) which enables us to collaborate on research-based projects, as well as the support of our partners for the touring version of the exhibition, Patrick Bourne at the Fine Art Society in London, and Jane Munro at the Fitzwilliam Museum at the University of Cambridge. I also extend thanks for their support to colleagues at the Ashmolean Museum, British Museum, National Maritime Museum, Tate Britain and especially those at the National Portrait Gallery. We are delighted that its Director, Sandy Nairne, is, most appropriately, opening the show here in Birmingham.

An exhibition is very much about teamwork and here at the Barber we have been supported by dedicated colleagues. I would particularly like to mention Chezzy Brownen whose efficiency and organisational skills have been invaluable with such a complex project. In addition on the administration side thanks go to Yvonne Locke, Rosemary Poynton, Richenda Roberts and Sophie Wilson who have worked closely together. We are indebted, on the technical front, to John Van Boolen and his team, including Stewart Meese, to the curatorial department under the leadership of Greg Smith, and Lionel Quigley and his team who have overseen the security arrangements. The remarkable storylines in this exhibition have been celebrated by our press and marketing officer Andrew Davies, the private view arrangements were made by Nemone Ryan and the musical interlude was organised by Colin Timms, Charles Brett and Joanne Sweet, whilst Kathryn Murray has devised the educational activities and Hannah Carroll has worked as research assistant. Thanks too to Tony Hollier for sourcing merchandise for the shop. It has been a great pleasure to work with Peter Owen on the design of both the catalogue and interpretation for the exhibition. Not to forget the interns who provide us with so much support, thanks go to Carly Hegenbarth, Natalie Osborne, Laura Pitcher, Holly Grange and Hannah Higham, also to our colleagues Tamsin Foulkes, Chris Mills and Maria Daniels. During a very busy period at the Barber, when we have been undergoing funding and staff reviews, I am most grateful to everyone who has demonstrated such enthusiastic and effective teamwork. The exhibition will, I am sure, be particularly popular, as it celebrates not only landscape painting and portraiture, but the values and ambitions of Victorian family life.

Professor Ann Sumner
Director, The Barber Institute of Fine Arts

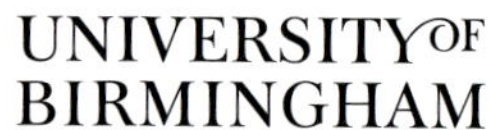

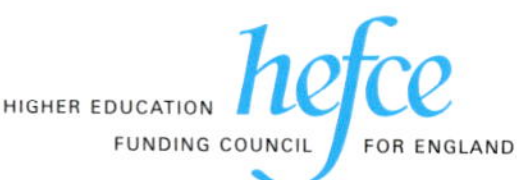

The Henry Barber Trust

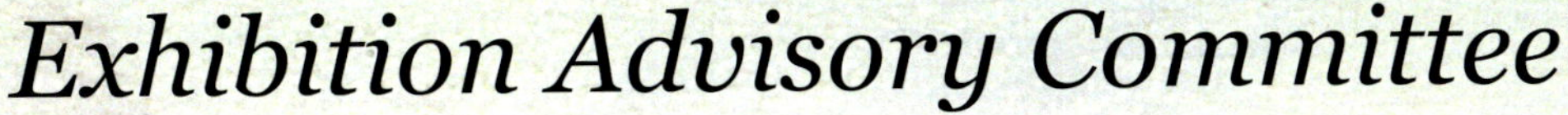

Exhibition Advisory Committee

Charles Brett

Christopher Gridley

Christiana Payne

Greg Smith (catalogue editor)

Paul Spencer-Longhurst

Ann Sumner

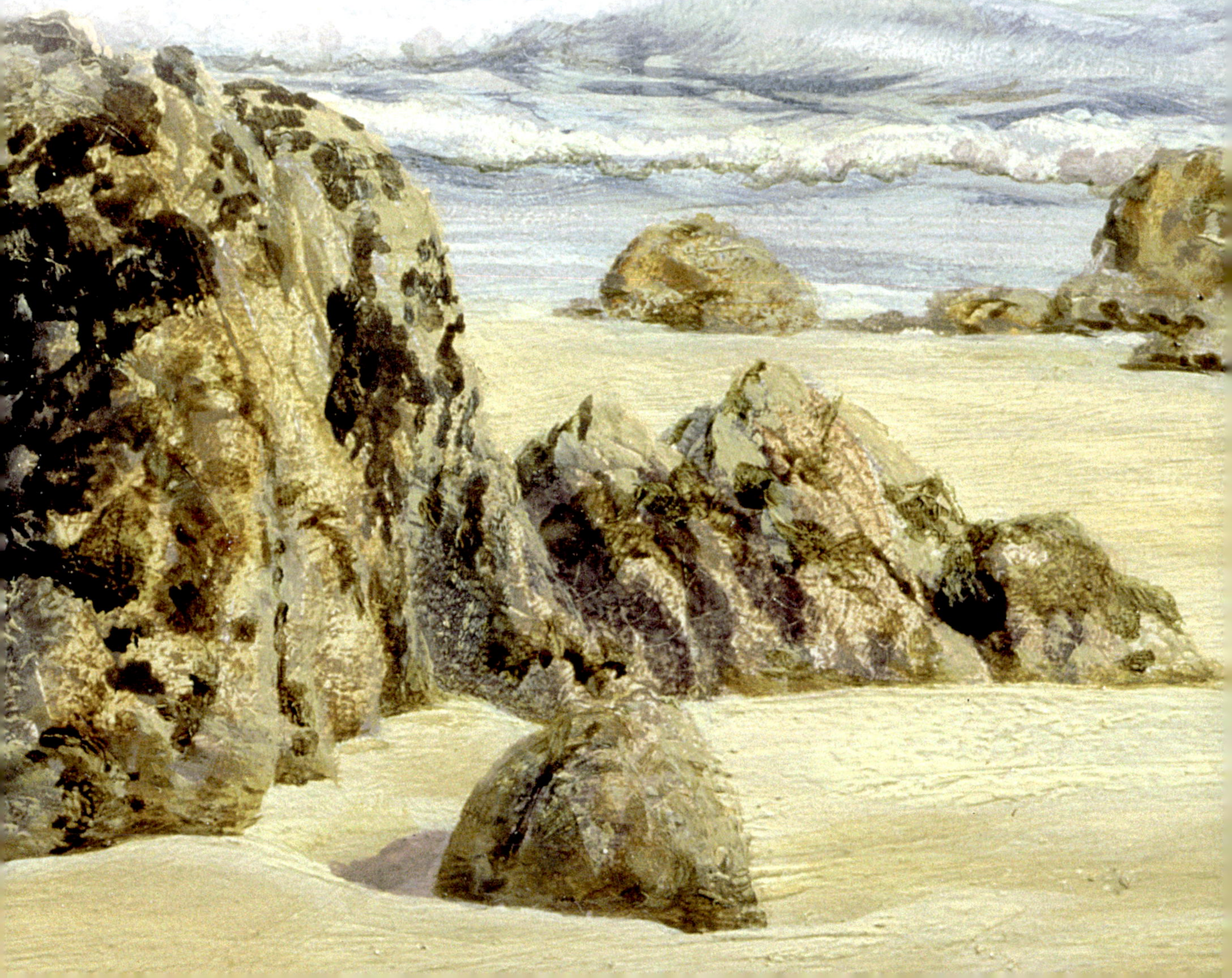

Acknowledgements

It has been a very enjoyable experience working on this exhibition and catalogue. I have particularly appreciated the friendliness and generosity of Brett's descendants, and the good humour and professionalism of the staff at the Barber Institute. I would like to thank the Arts and Humanities Research Council for supporting my research, and my colleagues at Oxford Brookes University for covering for my absences and providing general encouragement. Special thanks are due to Charles Brett, Christopher Gridley and Mike Hickox who have generously shared their knowledge of Brett's life and work, and provided much practical assistance, as well as a constant flow of stimulating ideas.

I am very grateful to all the lenders and to those who have helped and supported me in my research and contributed in various ways to the mounting of the exhibition. I would especially like to thank Nicholas Alfrey, Brian Allen, John d'Arcy, Nick and Liz Balaam, Patrick Bourne, Cécile Brett, Martin and Teresa Brett, Brian and Jenifer Brooke-Smith, Andrew and Christina Brownsword, Jeremy and Yvonne Clarke, Marie Considine (RBSA), David Cordingly, Colin Cruise, Caroline Dakers, Michael Day, Roy Fox, Peter Funnell, Adrian Gibbs of the Bridgeman Art Library, Colin Harrison, Rupert Maas, Jan Marsh, David McNeff, Lord Margadale, Joanna Martin, Guy Morrison, Jane Munro, Christopher Newall, Jenny Newall, Pamela Gerrish Nunn, Victoria Osborne, Peter Owen, Terence Pepper, Jim Pye, John Sansom, Jacob Simon, Susan Oliver, Kim Sloan, Sam Smiles, Alison Smith, Clare Smith, Gill, Jack and Peter Watson, Liz Woods, Aurelia Young and Charles Young. I would also like to pay tribute to my co-curator Ann Sumner, and to thank her for her vision and constant support which have kept the show on the road. And, last but not least, I want to thank Giles and Charlotte Payne, for making life worthwhile.

Dr Christiana Payne

Reader in History of Art at Oxford Brookes University

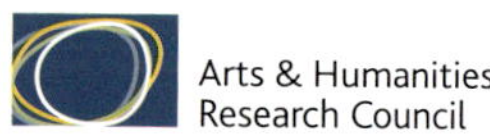

The Paul Mellon Centre *for Studies in British Art*

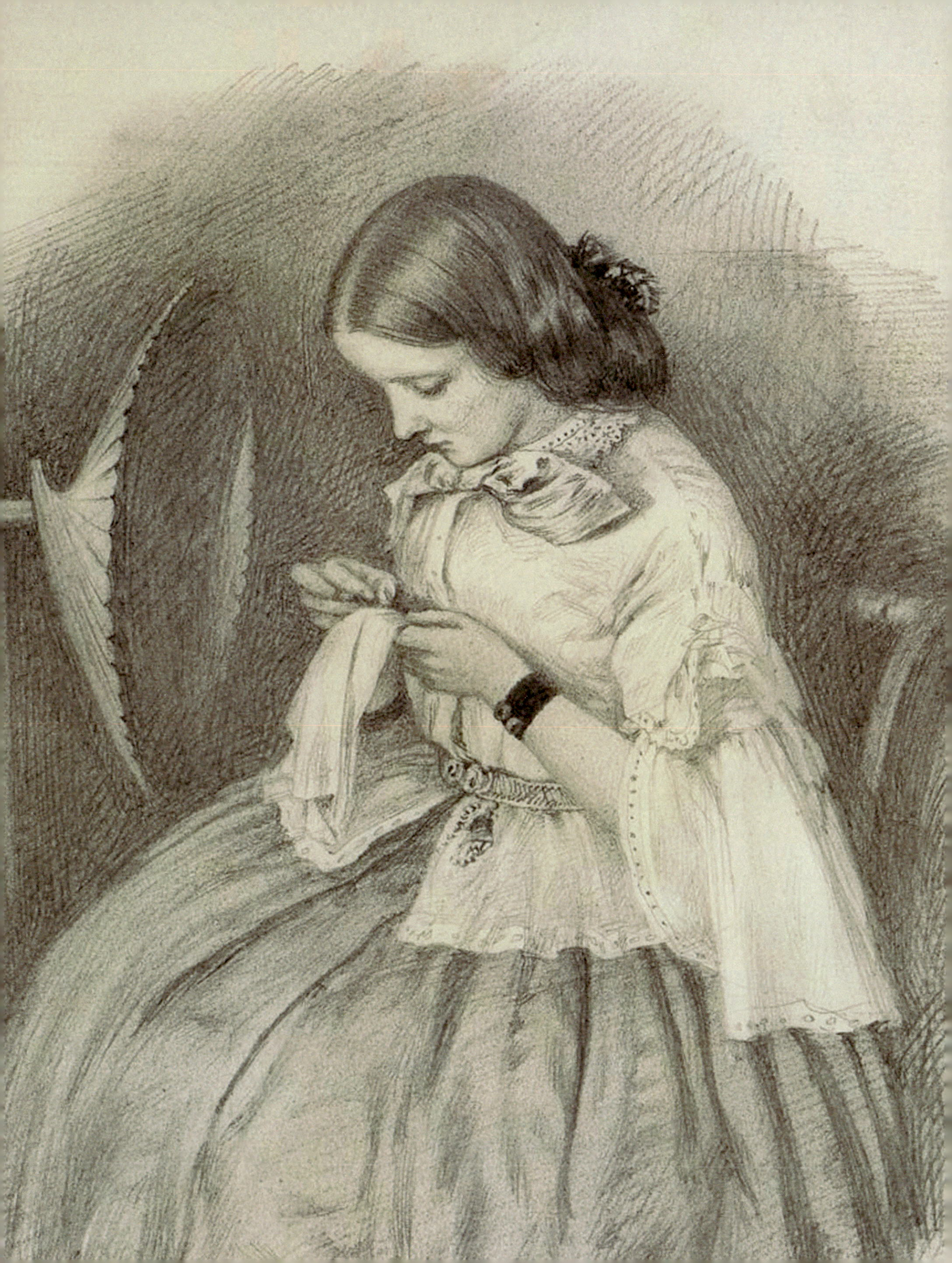

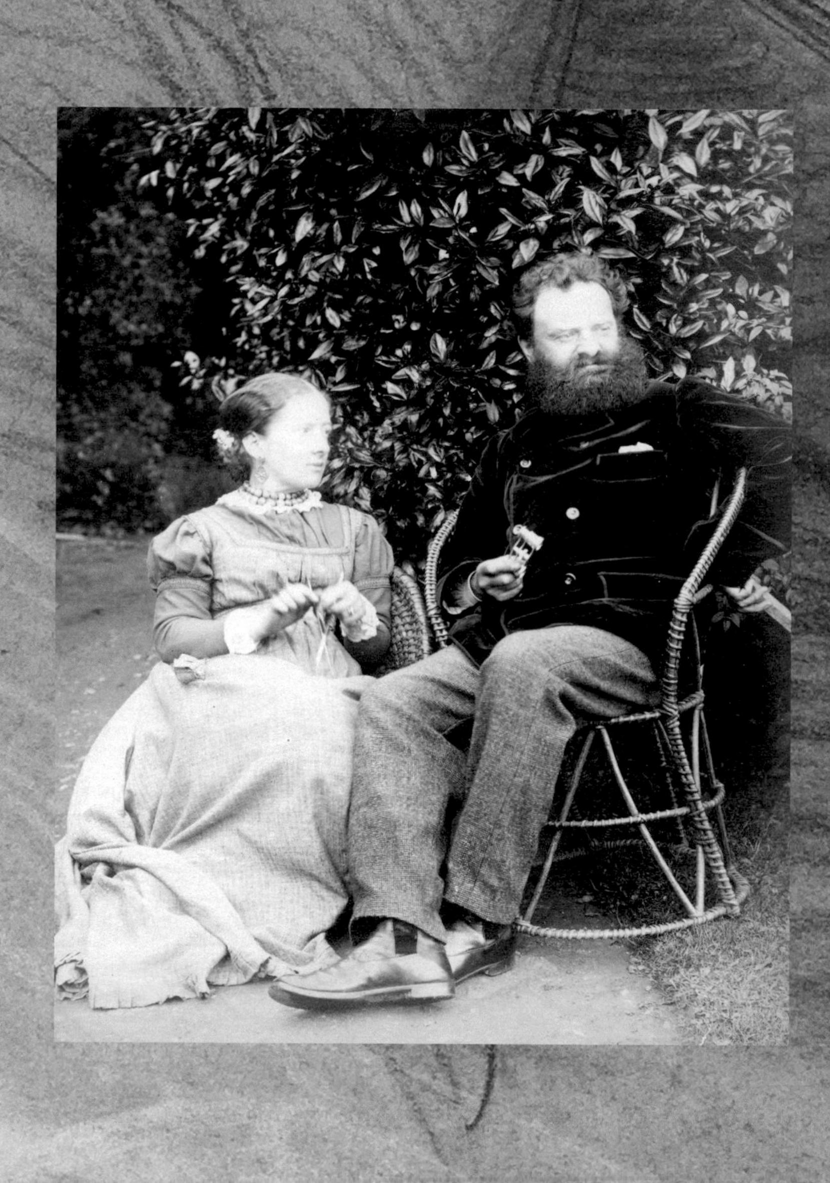

Opposite Page
John Brett, ***John and Mary Brett***
About 1878, photograph
Private collection
John holds binoculars, which he habitually used for painting the distances in his landscapes, while his industrious partner Mary appears to be knitting a sock.

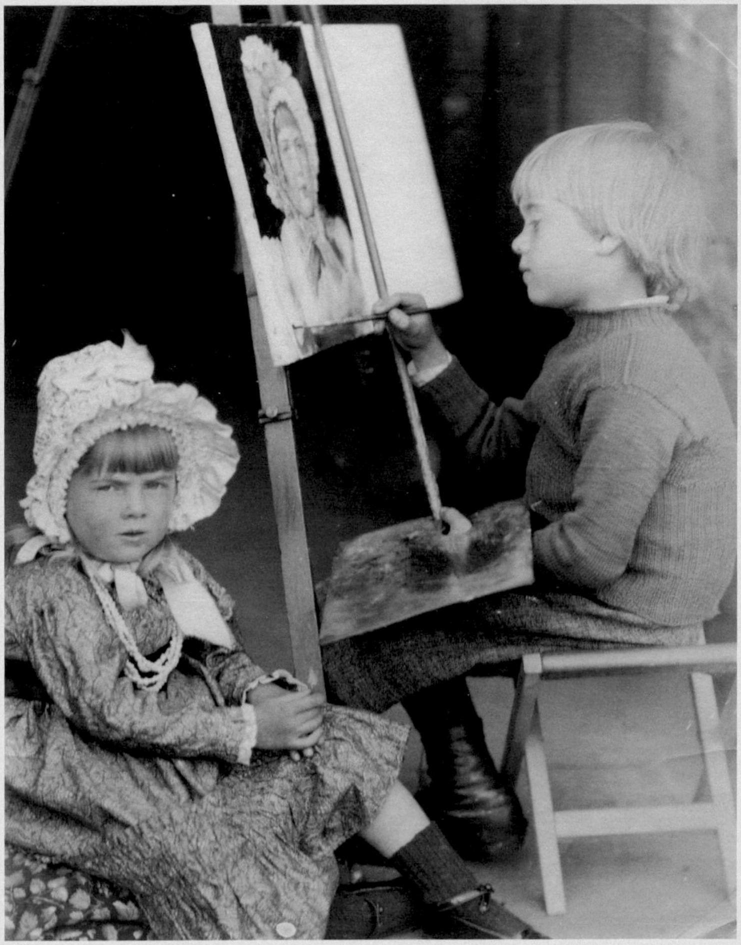

John Brett, ***Pansy Posing for Jasper***
1882, photograph
Private collection
In July 1882, while Brett was painting a portrait of his daughter Pansy, then aged four (no. 7), his older children took turns to sit or stand at the easel and be photographed. Eight-year-old Jasper seems to be taking the role particularly seriously.

John Brett began his experiments with photography in the late 1870s. The advent of gelatine dry plate negatives meant that images did not need to be processed immediately and photography consequently gained in popularity at this time. However, despite such technical advances, Brett still had to carry around boxes of glass plates and chemicals. The artist used the medium in a modern way, to record his growing family, often on their holidays. His son Michael was born in 1871, the first of seven children of whom Brett was very proud. They were photographed individually and in groups, often in carefully composed situations, but also swimming or carefree on the beach. Brett himself would sometimes appear in his photographs, rushing to join his family before the shutter came down. AS

Objects of Affection:
John Brett's Portraits

Christiana Payne

John Brett was a Pre-Raphaelite, that is, one of the group of artists in Victorian Britain who believed that art had begun to decay after the death of Raphael (1483 - 1520) and that it should be revitalised by returning to the close study of nature that had characterised Raphael's predecessors. The best-known members of this group were three of the original founders of the Pre-Raphaelite Brotherhood, formed in the autumn of 1848: John Everett Millais (1829 - 1896), William Holman Hunt (1827 - 1910) and Dante Gabriel Rossetti (1828 - 1882). The Brotherhood was of short duration, but its ideas had a profound impact on British art, and many artists working in the 1850s and 60s were designated as Pre-Raphaelites, either at the time or in retrospect. The hallmarks of the Pre-Raphaelite style were bright colours and minute finish. When painting people, they eschewed generalised features in favour of recording the peculiarities of individuals, and when producing landscapes, they aimed to work in the open air, recording every detail they could see instead of following repetitive formulae. John Brett became the most prominent landscape painter amongst the Pre-Raphaelites. In the late 1850s, his two great landscapes the *Stonebreaker* and *the Val d'Aosta* (figs. 1 and 2), earned the praise of John Ruskin, the art critic whose writings did much to establish the group as a force in British art. In later years Brett was less closely associated with Millais, Hunt and Rossetti, but his large, brightly coloured coastal scenes continued to keep the Pre-Raphaelite flame alive until the 1890s.

Although he made his name as a landscape painter, John Brett was interested in portraiture throughout his life. Apart from a pioneering article published by Mike Hickox in 1996, there has, however, been very little

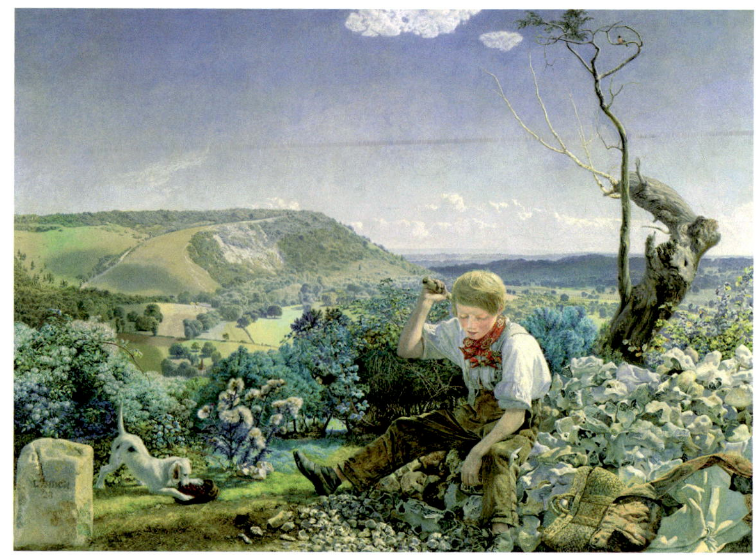

Fig. 1 John Brett, *Stonebreaker*
1857-8, oil on canvas
Walker Art Gallery, Liverpool

written on his portraits, an omission the present exhibition sets out to rectify.[1] In his youth Brett described the pleasure he experienced 'in striving to breathe a living soul into her form on the canvas', while at the very end of his career he wrote, 'There are few things men cherish more than the early portraits of their companions or their children. What we cannot hope to see repeated must obviously be beyond price'.[2] Most of Brett's surviving portraits were made for his own pleasure and kept in his possession to the end of his life, though there are records of others which were sold or given away and perhaps await rediscovery. His drawings are usually dated, and occasionally inscribed with his initials, but even when signed, they might well go unrecognised for Brett is not known as a portraitist. The emphasis on beauty and on delicate drawing which characterises Brett's landscapes is also found in his portraits. As a young man he made many portraits of his parents and his siblings, partly because they were always available as models, but also because he had a deep affection for them, which shines through in his writings. In middle life the emphasis shifted to friends and lovers, and particularly to beautiful women. Then in the 1870s, when he had a family of his own, he painted charming portraits of his offspring, but also transferred some of his energies to photography as a way of capturing the personalities of his 'marvellous children', arranging them in formal and informal groups, as well as making individual studies of them.

John Brett was born in 1831, the second eldest child of a family of five. His father, Charles Curtis Brett, was an army veterinary surgeon who had once served in the Royal Navy. In his youth, John spent much time with his older sister Rosa (born 1829), who was also a gifted artist, but one who never achieved her full potential, partly because of ill health, partly because of her gender. As the only daughter, family responsibilities weighed heavily on Rosa, although both John and their father encouraged her as much as they could. Then there were the three younger brothers: Theodore (born 1833), Arthur (1838), and Edwin (1841). Little is known of Theodore - it seems likely that he had a learning disability - but towards the younger two John adopted a paternal approach, taking a

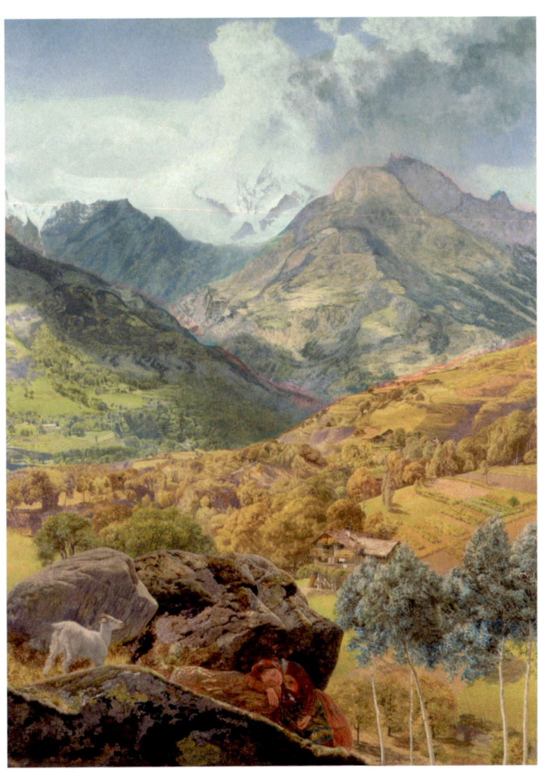

Fig. 2 John Brett, *Val d'Aosta*
1858, oil on canvas
Private collection

great interest in their education and career prospects. The family moved around England and Ireland with their father's regiment in the 1830s and early 1840s, until in 1846 they settled in Maidstone in Kent where they lived in a succession of rented houses. Brett's drawings and oil paintings of his parents and siblings reflect his keen sense of individual character; the energy and dignity of his father and the retiring nature of his mother, the impulsive, unbending personality of Rosa, and the chivalrous attitudes of Arthur and Edwin.

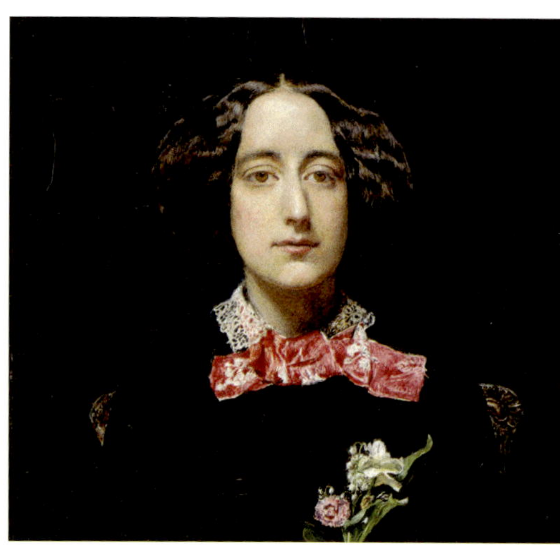

Fig. 3 John Everett Millais, *Emily Patmore*
1851, oil on panel
The Fitzwilliam Museum, University of Cambridge

A diary kept by Brett in the 1850s records his aspirations, his admiration for Pre-Raphaelitism, and his early attempts at portraiture. Hoping to be 'a great artist', he had set his sights on the Royal Academy with a view to training at the Academy Schools, showing his paintings and drawings in the annual exhibitions, and eventually becoming a member of the select body of Royal Academicians and Associates. He achieved the first of these aims in April 1853, after several attempts to produce a drawing from a cast of an antique sculpture. At the Academy Schools, the training was focused on the needs of the history painter; studying from the cast was followed by life drawing from nude models, and competitions encouraged young artists to develop multi-figure compositions. Despite the great reputation of Turner, who had died just two years earlier, landscape painters were accorded a lower status than figure painters, and John Brett recorded his misgivings that it might be wrong to pass by 'the most powerful instrument for the conveyance of absolute thought at the command of the artist: viz the human being.'[3]

This early diary also records some of John Brett's first attempts at portraiture, which were generally commissions from family members and close friends. In 1852 he painted the mother of a friend, Mrs Hall, partly from life and partly from two daguerrotypes, but this was unsatisfactory as they were 'as unlike each other as different people' and she was 'at times … so unlike herself that I should scarcely recognise her', and he found it hard to get a good expression.[4] The diary does not mention the use of daguerrotypes again. Another portrait which cost him much pain, despite many sittings, was one of the Congregationalist minister Edward White. Brett had great admiration for White but wrote, 'I always find it very difficult to get a resemblance', and after four months of intermittent work on the portrait concluded that he could do nothing with it because 'it was so bad'.[5] More successful was a portrait of a baby, Arthur Marriott, which Brett presented to the child's father, the Reverend Edward Marriott, vicar of Fernhurst in Sussex.[6] Brett was fervently religious at this stage in his life, and a hint of the high ideals he brought to portraiture can be seen in his description in October 1852 of a face he had seen at a meeting: 'I saw beaming in a human face more of Divine love & the purity of restored nature - The seal of the angel, than I ever beheld, it was truly one of the children of light, it was her sister, it was my own … deeply has that pure image impressed itself on my soul'.[7]

As a student in London, Brett went regularly to the soirées hosted by Eliza Orme, who was the sister-in-law of his aunt Caroline. He described Eliza as the 'fountain head' of most of his introductions: her friends included the young Pre-Raphaelites John Everett Millais, Thomas Woolner and Dante Gabriel Rossetti, as well as Rossetti's brother and sister, the art critic William Michael Rossetti and the poet Christina Rossetti.[8] It was through Eliza that Brett met her sister, Emily, and Emily's husband, the poet Coventry Patmore.[9] It was Patmore who introduced Brett to William Holman Hunt, and this circle also included the art critic John Ruskin, who was to play a major part in Brett's life. It seems that Brett acquired a reputation at Mrs Orme's for portrait sketches, as he mentions in his diary that, 'Of late I have also found myself benefited in drawing by these visits by having as I usually do to sketch the portrait of some member of the family or visitor & this in a short time & in presence of others is good practice'.[10] None of these rapid sketches can currently be identified, but it is intriguing to think who some of these 'visitors' might have been. In making quick sketches of people at parties, Brett was following the example of Millais, who enjoyed making rapid studies and presenting them to his hostess.[11] Two years later Brett made a chalk drawing of Coventry Patmore which was used as the frontispiece to his *Memoirs and Correspondence*, published in 1900. Writing to F. G. Stephens in 1896, Brett said it was 'considered very like him, but Rossetti said it was prettified'.[12] It is clear from Brett's diary that he felt slightly uncomfortable at the Ormes', unwilling to be a flatterer or a hanger-on to the fringes of a group, and perhaps disturbed by the jealousies and rivalries within the Pre-Raphaelites. On one occasion he wrote in his diary 'If I cant form the centre of a circle never let me be the fag end of one.'[13]

Early Pre-Raphaelitism aimed at strict truth to nature, and in portraiture this meant resisting the temptation to idealise the

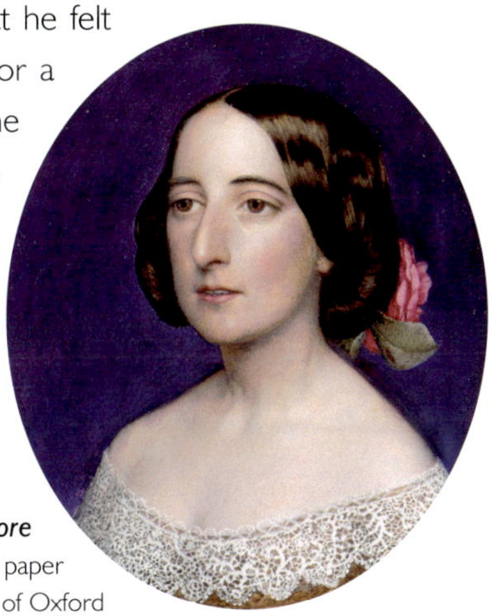

Fig. 4 John Brett, *Emily Patmore*
1856, watercolour on paper
The Ashmolean Museum, University of Oxford

features of the sitter. Millais's portrait of Emily Patmore (fig. 3) is a prime example of this approach. It is justly celebrated as a work which boldly ignores the usual tendency to flatter the sitter in line with current ideas of female beauty, presenting, instead, a keenly observed portrayal of an intelligent individual. Emily's husband Coventry, however, was not impressed. Writing to F. G. Stephens much later, after Emily had died, he declared that it 'omitted all the refinement of her face ... I keep it locked up as I do not like the children to think it like their mother.'[14] Brett also told Stephens that Patmore 'hated Millais' portrait of his wife beyond speech'.[15] By this time Emily was a legend, known as the inspiration for Coventry Patmore's famous poem, *The Angel in the House*, which came to be regarded as the blueprint for perfect womanly behaviour. A focus on imperfections was not likely to please either the sitters or their loved ones, and it could be seen as incompatible with the objective of bringing out the essence of a person's character. Millais gradually modified this aspect of Pre-Raphaelitism in his portraits, and it is likely that John Brett did the same.

Brett's drawing of Eliza Orme (no. 9), which probably dates from 1854 or 1855, is honest (as far as we can tell) in its presentation of her low forehead, large nose and double chin; but his painting of Emily, exhibited at the Royal Academy in 1856 (fig. 4), uses a large area of décolletage to set off her nose, diverting attention instead to her dark eyes and slender neck. This portrait was one of the first three works he showed at the Royal Academy. It has only been discovered recently that it is not an oil painting but a heavily varnished watercolour. Brett was very fond of Emily Patmore, whom he met when he first came to London. He first mentions her in his diary on 30 October 1852, when he notes that he 'saw Mrs P. and had a long & agreable chat.'[17] It is very likely that Emily would have shown Brett the poem Robert Browning had inscribed in her album just a couple of weeks earlier, *A Face*. This poem imagines a portrait of her painted in profile against a gold background, in the manner of the Florentine artists of the fifteenth century: 'No shade encroaching on the matchless mold / Of those two lips, which should be opening soft ... her lithe neck, three fingers might surround / How it should waver on the pale gold ground / Up to the fruit-shaped, perfect chin it lifts!'[18] Brett's portrait succeeds in capturing some of this 'refinement' that Coventry had found lacking in Millais's work. In addition, Brett's studies at the Academy in these years would have directed him towards the idealised forms of antique sculpture, and it is probable that he was also studying

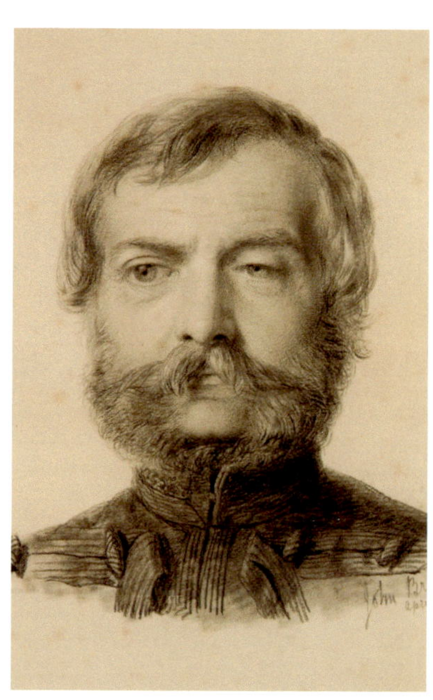

Fig. 5 John Brett, *Charles Curtis Brett*
1855, pencil and chalk on paper
Private collection

Old Master drawings in the British Museum, where Patmore worked, and looking at the drawn portraits of his contemporaries, such as George Richmond (1809 - 1896).

1855 appears to have been a key year in Brett's development as a portraitist and it is unfortunate that his diary for this year (if he kept one) has not survived. He made a series of very delicately executed portrait drawings in fine pencil and chalk. Three of these drawings, of his father, mother and sister Rosa, were made in quick succession on 7, 13 and 14 April (fig. 5). They have remained in the Brett family, and the discoloration of the paper shows that for many years they must have been framed and hung on the wall, with the drawing of Rosa, in an oval mount, probably being placed between her parents whose portraits were in circular mounts. At the end of the same year he made another meticulous pencil drawing of his brother Arthur (no. 10). In all these works Brett shows a real mastery of technique. His portraits are generally more successful when he concentrates on the head alone, and in graphic media he was, at this stage, much more skilled than he was in oils.

As a student at the Academy, Brett would have been made to concentrate on drawing from sculpture from January 1853 until December 1854, when he was first admitted to draw from the living model in the Life School. Hardly any of his studies of sculpture for this period have survived, but it is clear from his diary entries that he took a close interest in drawing materials and techniques. On Christmas Day 1852 he describes a drawing he had done 'executed without strokes the shades being stumped with carbon and stippled up with chalk which has a very beautiful silvery transparent effect.'[19] Two months later he writes of a drawing being 'stippled up to very elaborate finish with conté over a stumping of carbon on Wolf's paper.'[20] With the use of these methods he was able to achieve incredibly fine definition and shading in his early portrait drawings, so it appeared that a soul had indeed been breathed onto the paper as he had described it earlier in his career.[21] Unsurprisingly, he notes that his fellow students remarked on 'the peculiarity of my style' and the 'elaborateness of my finish'.[22] Brett was

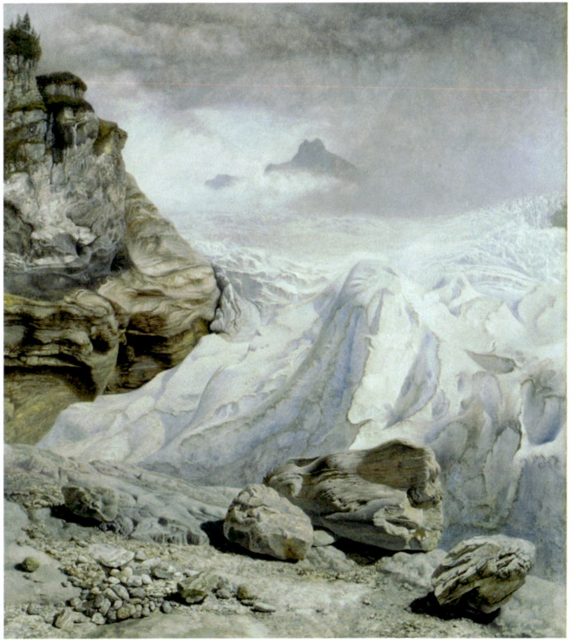

Fig. 6 John Brett, *The Glacier of Rosenlaui*
1856, oil on canvas
Tate Britain, London

scientifically minded - in his early years he was uncertain whether he should choose astronomy or art for his career - and he had plans to develop a new improved chalk for drawing:

> *I have lately had schemes in my head for improving charcoal for pencil Drawings, by uniting it with lead, an experiment of precipitation by galvanic current of acetate of lead on finely powdered animal charcoal - failed for want of the requisite pressure to give it solidity & I intend trying to saturate the charcoal in its natural condition & then to precipitate it.*[23]

The 1855 drawings of Rosa and his parents (fig. 5) are in a mixture of media - graphite with chalk - and it is possible that he also used a crayon which blended carbon and lead. In 1856 Brett made his debut as an exhibitor at the Royal Academy, with one or perhaps two of these fine drawings, along with the watercolour portrait of Emily Patmore. There was an established tradition of showing meticulously executed portrait drawings at the Academy which has recently been explored in the exhibition, *The Intimate Portrait*.[24] It is unlikely that any of Brett's exhibits were for sale, but he probably hoped that they would lead to commissions for further portraits.

Having kept a very detailed diary between late 1851 and the summer of 1854, Brett made only intermittent entries during the crucial years when he was closest to the original members of the Pre-Raphaelite Brotherhood - or else he kept a fuller record, which has since been lost or destroyed.[25] In the summer of 1856 he went to Switzerland, where he painted his first great landscape *The Glacier of Rosenlaui* (fig. 6). There he met another Pre-Raphaelite follower, John William Inchbold, whose methods he found deeply inspiring. On his return, Dante Gabriel Rossetti admired the painting and took it to show to Ruskin.[26] In May 1857, two watercolours by Brett were included in the first Pre-Raphaelite group exhibition, held at 4 Russell Place, Fitzroy Square, and they were reviewed favourably by Coventry Patmore, who said they were 'wonders of laborious and effective finish'.[27] Some of Brett's works also went with other Pre-Raphaelite paintings to New York, Philadelphia and Boston between October 1857 and June 1858. In the summer of 1857 he was at Mickleham in Surrey, painting the *Stonebreaker* (fig. 1). The enigmatic, unfinished portrait of Christina Rossetti (no. 1) probably dates from this time. There is significant circumstantial evidence that the two came close to an engagement in that year. Either he proposed and she turned him down, or he never proposed and she was left feeling hurt.[28] Brett's diary entries for earlier and later years reveal a strong propensity to fall in love combined with a desire to avoid 'entanglements', so either scenario is possible. Whatever happened, the portrait remained unfinished and, although Brett kept on friendly terms with William Michael Rossetti, Dante Gabriel was scathing about him in later years.[29] Hunt continued to be a good friend until 1863, when the two men fell out over the arrangements for the exhibition of works rejected by the Royal Academy, including two landscapes by Brett.[30] The portrait of Christina is thoroughly Pre-Raphaelite in its use of bright colour - including ultramarine, applied to a white ground - its very fine brushwork and its adoption of a format that recalls Elizabethan miniatures. The feather in the background may owe something to John Ruskin's advice to artists to study Albrecht Dürer. In the same year, 1857, Brett drew a self portrait which is very reminiscent of Dürer and is even inscribed in German 'mein selbst (ganz wahr)' - 'my self (quite true)'.[31]

We do not know when Brett first met John Ruskin. Brett records his admiration for Ruskin's writings in his diary in May 1852, and he probably would have had opportunities to meet him through the Patmores or the Ormes, but, as late as December 1856, they either had not met or Brett did not know Ruskin well enough to show him the *Glacier* himself. By April 1858, when Ruskin praised the *Stonebreaker* publicly in his *Academy Notes*, they were on friendly terms and Ruskin knew that Brett's next destination was the Valle d'Aosta in Piedmont. Here Brett painted his masterpiece, the most completely Pre-Raphaelite landscape painting, the *Val d'Aosta* (fig. 2). Another fine self portrait (no. 12) probably records its completion: both self portraits are in pen and ink, a medium which requires great assurance since no erasure is possible, and record his high forehead and intense gaze. But even in December 1858, when he felt confident that the *Val d'Aosta* would sell for £450 and Ruskin had praised it 'enough already to make me happy and Father and Rosa proud through what he has said of it', Brett was contemplating a career as a figure painter: 'it is as I plan at present my last landscape'. In the same breath he records that he has just begun a 'small full length of Edwin in oil' (fig. 7).[32]

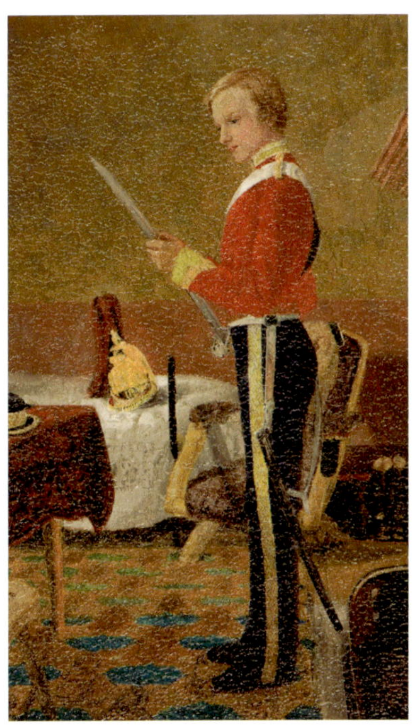

Fig. 7 John Brett, *Edwin Brett (detail)*
1859, oil on board
Private collection

In 1859 Brett worked intensively on figure compositions. He made many designs for subjects from literature, probably hoping that he might get work as an illustrator as well as collecting ideas for paintings to be shown at the Royal Academy. The full-length portrait of Edwin was followed by an oil portrait of his brother Arthur (no. 2), painted against a heraldic background which underlined his similarity to his namesake, the great King Arthur, recently celebrated by the poet Tennyson in his *Idylls of the King*. Brett's exhibition picture for that year was *The Hedger* (fig. 8), a landscape with a prominent figure, and Brett prepared himself for this painting by making a very detailed drawing (no. 16). In the autumn and winter of 1859/60 Brett made many drawings, mostly in pen and ink, of women engaged in various domestic activities; reading, writing letters and sewing (no. 21). The meticulous technique recalls the illustrations of Millais, an artist whom Brett greatly admired, and the subject matter can be related to Coventry Patmore's poem, *The Angel in the House*, inspired by his wife Emily. At the end of the year Brett made a series of very fine pen and ink drawings of family members, perhaps to celebrate his complete command of the medium, as he had done with the chalk drawings of April 1855. The drawings of his mother and father and Georgina Hannay, soon to become Arthur's wife (nos. 17-19), were all done in a period of four days between 27 and 30 December, when the family were together (except for Edwin) to celebrate Christmas and New Year.

John Ruskin would have approved of Brett's concentration on pen and ink. In a letter written in 1863, he advised Brett to make 'quantities of black and white studies', arguing that 'Millais' highest results have been got at through pen and ink - so Rossetti - so Jones. There is no hope for anybody but in the inkbottle.'[33] However, Ruskin did not approve of Brett's attempts to gain recognition as a painter of the human figure. In his review of the *Stonebreaker*, he concentrated entirely on the landscape and made no reference to the figure. He advised the collector Thomas Plint not to buy *The Hedger* (fig. 8), writing that the subject was 'wholly uninteresting'.[34] And in the same letter in which he recommends black and white studies he tells Brett: 'You know - you lost no end of time by that accursed fit of hankering after being a figure painter, that took you; so the landscape had all that to suffer from as well.'[35] Ruskin's father, John James, had a different view. He seems to have taken a paternal interest in Brett, inviting him to dinner regularly and buying paintings from him.

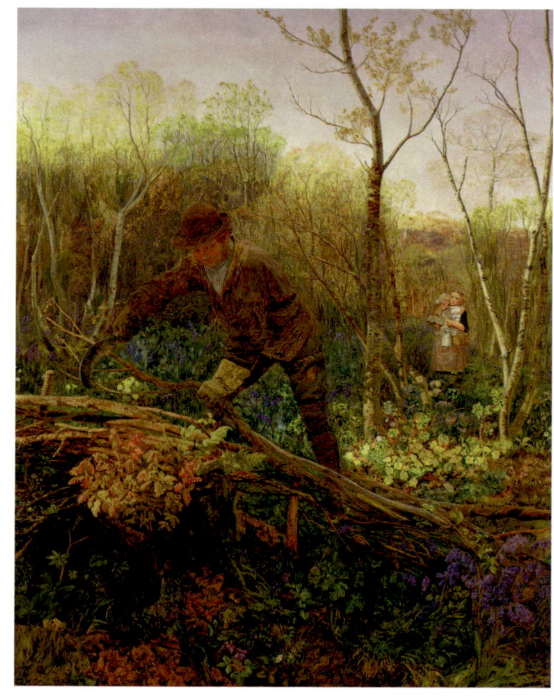

Fig. 8 John Brett, *The Hedger*
1859-60, oil on canvas
Private collection

He declined to buy *The Hedger* with its foreground of 'wood Hyacinths' (bluebells), but agreed to guarantee its purchaser, the dealer William Vokins, against loss, and he evidently appreciated Brett's portrait drawings:

> *I should also be quite obliged to you to spare me £20 worth of sketches, however slight, including the Lovely Lady of Florence for in Human Countenance your great Strength lies forgive me ye wood Hyacinths and all the other beauties of your marvellous Foreground.*[36]

This comment suggest that John James had seen many portrait drawings by Brett, perhaps including some which are now lost. It was, perhaps, no coincidence that Ruskin fell out with Brett in the summer of 1864, a few months after John James Ruskin died. There is no evidence of any further contact between them, although Brett continued to admire Ruskin and to buy his books.

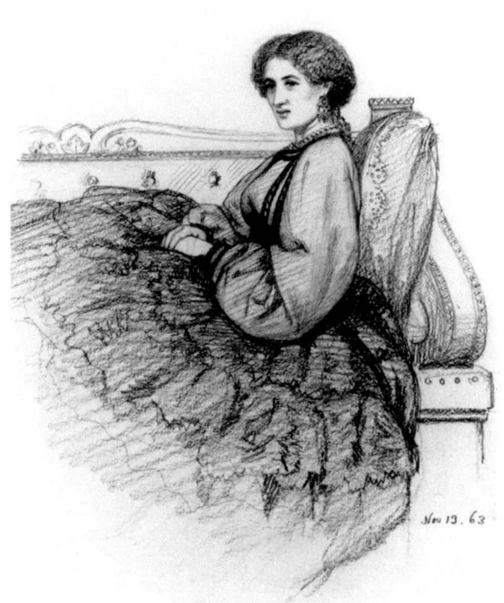

Fig. 9 John Brett, *Jeannette Loeser*
1863, pencil on paper
Private collection

The 'Lovely Lady of Florence' referred to in John James Ruskin's letter was probably Jeannette Loeser, a woman Brett met in Florence in the spring of 1863. The true nature of their relationship is unknown, but the obsessive and seductive character of his drawings of her suggests a love affair. He spent two winters with her and her companion, the musician Jacques Blumenthal, in Capri and Rome in 1863/4 and 1864/5. During the second winter they were joined by the singer Georgina Weldon, who kept a diary which vividly records the jealousies provoked by her presence, providing further circumstantial evidence that Brett and Jeannette were lovers. On one occasion Jeannette warned Georgina that Brett was 'a dangerous seducteur'.[37] Brett's drawings of Jeannette (fig. 9, nos. 26 and 36) are reminiscent of Dante Gabriel Rossetti's drawings of Lizzie Siddal and Jane Morris. In her physiognomy, she was not unlike Jane Morris, with voluminous hair, dark eyes and a sumptuous profile. There are many drawings of her in his sketchbooks (no. 36), and many single sheets which he obviously kept, since they remained in the family collections. None of these is inscribed with her name. There must be others which he gave to Jeannette or sold to collectors like John James Ruskin.

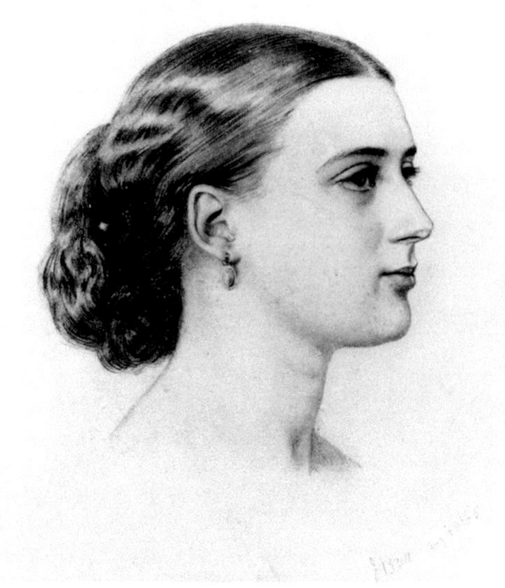

Fig. 10 John Brett, *Georgina Weldon*
1866, pencil on paper
Private collection

Jeannette Loeser was the sitter for the only full-length portrait which Brett ever exhibited, the *Lady with a Dove* (no. 3), which was finished in August 1864 and exhibited at the Royal Manchester Institution in the autumn of 1865. Women with doves are ubiquitous in the art, literature and music of this period, and there are several possible sources of inspiration. Poems by Tennyson and Browning, a novel by Nathaniel Hawthorne, and a hymn by Mendelssohn all offer significant precedents, and artists who treated similar themes include Millais, Alexander Munro and John Frederick Lewis. Usually the beauty of a woman is compared to that of the bird (an idea Brett had used in his placement of a feather in the background of his portrait of Christina Rossetti) and the implication is that the woman is also dove-like in character, that is, gentle, submissive and faithful. Occasionally, however, women are compared to caged birds who would rather be wild, in a recognition of the constraints on women's behaviour imposed by the strict moral codes of Victorian society.[38] Brett seems to have had rather liberal attitudes to the role of women, and it is significant that the dove in the portrait is not restrained in any way. Perhaps the painting should not be considered a portrait at all: it did not end up in the possession of either Jeannette Loeser or Jacques Blumenthal, as one might expect, and Brett referred to it as 'the picture of the Lady and the pigeon' when writing to its eventual purchaser, Alfred Morrison.[39] It is possible that he intended to give it to Jeannette as a gift, but if this was the case he must have taken it back when their relationship broke up in March 1865.

Brett's correspondence with Alfred Morrison suggests that he saw some of his paintings and drawings - especially those of beautiful women - as objects which would be of interest to collectors, rather than portraits of individuals to be bought by the sitters themselves or their friends or relations. Morrison was a very rich man whose art collection contained many portraits from earlier historical periods. The 1860s was the decade of the Aesthetic Movement, when the depiction of beauty for its own sake was taking over from the pursuit of truth as the primary aim of many artists connected with Pre-Raphaelitism. In August 1866 Brett wrote to Morrison: 'I have been trying this morning to make a likeness of a beautiful Lady. If it succeeds you shall see it. It is only a little pencil drawing but if I can make it sufficiently beautiful I think of painting her.'[40] On the afternoon of the same day he visited the National Portrait Gallery with the 'beautiful Lady' - Georgina Weldon (fig. 10) - and her husband. Five days later he wrote another letter to Morrison in which he offered some general remarks on portraiture, which were obviously part of a continuing conversation:

> *I don't think that the remnants of portraiture every day seen at the Academy can be dignified with the name of a school, since they are only remarkable for the absence of any characteristic quality, nor do I see any chance of improvement till the subject comes to be regarded with greater seriousness by those who give commissions and by those who sit. And the teachings of the puritans and spiritualists who have brought the visible and the tangible into contempt must be forgotten before that feeling can grow up.*[41]

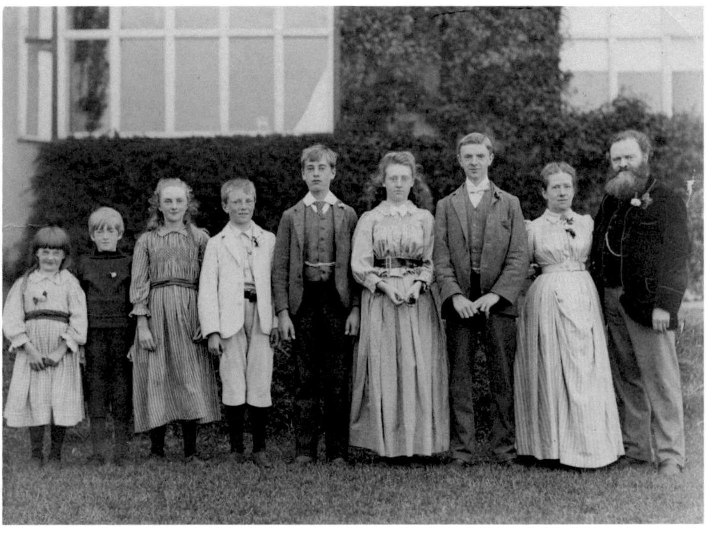

Fig. 11 John Brett, *The Brett Family*
1890, photograph
Private collection

Brett's strictures on 'puritans and spiritualists' probably refers to those writers who had argued that art should not simply record visible appearances, but aim at an idealised beauty which would convey the soul of the sitter. By this stage in his life Brett's early religious fervour had given way to a more sceptical and agnostic approach, and he may also have meant to refer to the influence of religion in general. The letter suggests that Brett was thinking about getting more seriously involved in portraiture himself. Perhaps he was simply hoping for portrait commissions from Morrison: in July 1868 a receipt shows that he had done an oil portrait of Mrs Morrison, two pencil heads of her, and an etching of Mr Morrison.[42] These four works (all currently untraced) were in addition to the chalk drawing of Alfred in this exhibition (no. 33).

Brett made many drawings of Georgina Weldon in the late summer, autumn and winter of 1866, finally starting his oil portrait on 23 December. Georgina's diary for that period records 24 visits from Brett, and specifically mentions him sketching her on most of those occasions (no. 29). She also records receiving letters from Brett on 12 occasions, and writing to him on a further nine. At the present time, none of these letters, and only a few of the drawings, are known to survive. On 29 August she writes in her shorthand that Brett is inclined to fall in love with her: 'it is most distressing'.[43] Clearly, Brett's interest in Georgina was not purely aesthetic. Yet he writes of these portrait drawings to Morrison in a way which suggests a higher aim, one that is reminiscent of his diary entry about the 'Divine love & the purity of restored nature' that he had seen in a woman's face in 1852:

> *The Lady I am trying to draw is one of those subjects where complete success is alone of value, the expression at particular moments reaching a Divine beauty which if one cant get one fails utterly.*[44]

The oil portrait of Georgina was never finished and may have been destroyed. After John, Edwin and Rosa spent Christmas with Georgina and Harry Weldon in 1867 and they were all 'very merry', she decided that the Bretts were 'a 'orrid wulgar lot' and John himself 'odious'. In June 1868 he was still trying to get Georgina to sit for her portrait, but she refused.[45]

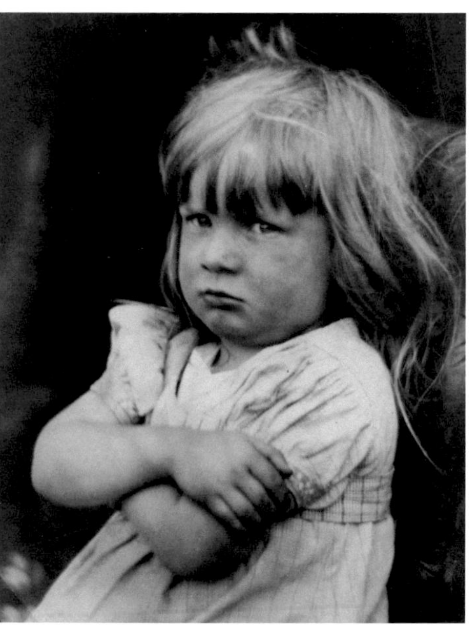

Fig. 12 John Brett, *Alfred Brett*
About 1878, photograph
Private collection

We do not know whether Georgina's portrait was full-length, but the amount of time Brett spent on it suggests that it might have been. Drawings of Mrs Morrison (no. 32) and of Ottilie Blind from this period show that he drew their head and shoulders at the top of a piece of paper, as if he intended to fill in more of the body later. He continued to make lovely drawings of friends throughout the 1860s, but the difficulties of painting the whole of the human figure may have deterred him from taking up commissioned portraiture. He may also have decided that portraiture was not sufficiently lucrative. For the oil portrait of Mrs Morrison, two drawings and an etching he received £128, but at the same period Morrison was prepared to pay £600 for a seascape.[47] It was also in the late 1860s that Brett did his last detailed watercolours; as with portraits, he may have decided that the intensive work needed for a detailed drawing simply was not worth it.

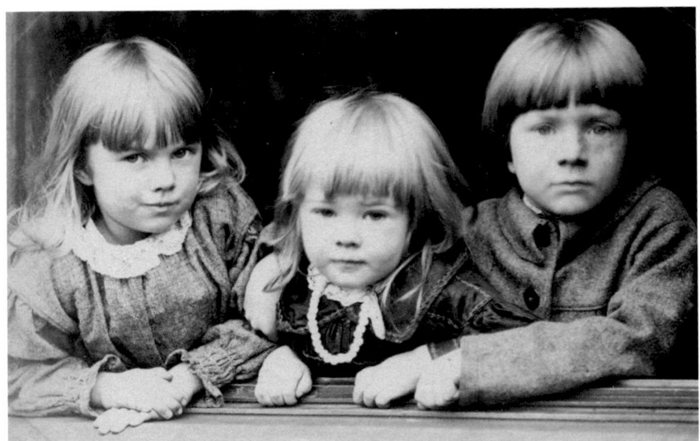

Fig. 13 John Brett, *Pansy, Spencer and Alfred*
About 1883, photograph
Private collection

In 1870 John Brett's life changed: a holiday he later referred to as a 'honeymoon' with Mary Ann Howcroft was followed nine months later by the birth of his first child, Michael.[48] Then, in quick succession came Daisy (born 1873), Jasper (1874), Alfred (1876), Pansy (1878), Spencer (1880) and Gwendolen (1882, fig. 11). Although there is no evidence that John and Mary were ever married, he settled happily into the role of a family man, taking his children for long summer holidays by the coast and showing a great interest in their individual personalities and achievements. He became a prolific painter of seascapes and coastal scenes, and also developed his interests in astronomy, architecture and sailing. Brett took an active part in the design of the two family houses built for him in Putney by the Birmingham firm of Martin and Chamberlain, 6 Keswick Road (1877) and Daisyfield (1887-9). Both houses had innovative features, including open plans, central heating and burglar alarms, as well as flat roofs to accommodate his telescopes. For a few years in the early 1880s, the family spent their summer holidays on a large yacht, the *Viking*, which also served as a floating studio.

Brett painted a few portraits of his family (nos. 5-8), but now his main mode of recording them took the form of photography. He had always been interested in science and technology; also, with his very precisely finished style, he may have found that the difficulties involved in getting small children to pose were insurmountable. In 1879, John and Mary began a family diary, entitled 'Memoranda of the Early Travels of our Children', and the first entry records that photography is 'at present the particular divine service set apart in this establishment for Sundays'.[49] The first family photographs appear to date from 1878. Over the next 12 years Brett took many photographs of his children, individually or in groups. He was justifiably proud of their health and beauty: indeed, the novelist George Eliot, who met the family in 1878, commented that they were 'fit to eat.'[50] His photographs are carefully composed, sometimes showing the influence of Julia Margaret Cameron, occasionally reaching a degree of apparent informality and naturalness which makes them look very modern.

An early photograph of Alfred, known as Doll, captures the irrepressibility of a toddler (fig. 12). Brett wrote of him in 1883, when he was six: 'Doll drinks in the enjoyment of his little life in deep draughts and his beautiful wild song in the minor key is a delightful welcome to the day whenever the sun rises.'[51] It was probably in 1883 that he took group photographs of Alfred and Pansy with Spencer, whom he said was 'too beautiful for a photograph to represent: the clear pearliness of his complexion and the archness of his manners and expression being past reproduction' (fig. 13).[52] As they got older, Brett chose poses which conveyed the particular abilities and predilections of each child. Jasper, whose eyes of 'supernatural keenness' Brett marvelled at in 1879, was by 1889 regularly bringing back the drawing prizes from school, and Brett's portrait study of him shows him painting, with an expression which conforms to what his father saw as his 'good, gentle nature' (fig. 14).[53] Around this time Brett delighted in lining up the whole family to show the 'curve' of their relative heights (fig. 11).

By the end of his life Brett had amassed a rich archive of the faces of those who had meant the most to him, from his younger siblings in their childhood, through the friends, lovers and fellow artists he knew in his middle years, to his own children as they grew from babyhood to adolescence. His methods and techniques varied, but the aims remained remarkably consistent: to record appearances, but always with an eye to youthful beauty, character and expression. The works in this exhibition are drawn mainly from those which remained in the family collections after Brett's death. However, it is to be hoped that their display, and the publication of the catalogue, will bring to light others which passed into the hands of their sitters, or other purchasers, during Brett's lifetime. While he never became a professional portraitist, a survey of his work in this area might lead many to agree with John James Ruskin that he had great strengths in the depiction of the 'Human Countenance'.

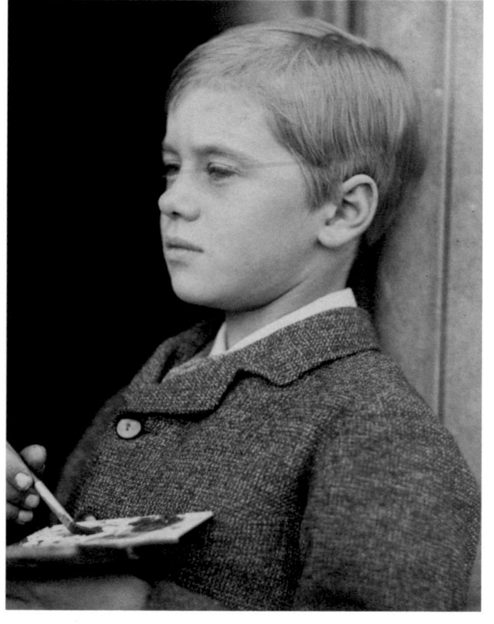

Fig. 14 John Brett, *Jasper Brett*
About 1888, photograph
Private collection

Notes

1. Hickox 1996 and 1998.

2. JBD, 31 March 1852, p. 9; Brett 1899, p. 828.

3. JBD, 20 October 1853, p. 47.

4. JBD, 22 April 1852, p. 12.

5. JBD, 18 May 1853, p. 37; 17 August 1853, p. 44.

6. JBD, 27 January 1853, p. 26.

7. JBD, 23 October 1852, p. 19.

8. 'During this season [January 1852] a few visits were made to the existing exhibitions & to that fountain head of most of my introductions the Ormes' (JBD, 3 April 1852, p. 10).

9. In a letter to Frederick George Stephens, another of the original Pre-Raphaelite Brothers, Brett wrote 'I came up to London in 1852 or earlier ... Immediately on arrival I was kindly entertained by the Ormes. There I met Mrs Patmore who became a great friend of mine and remained so ... Mrs Orme was the leading spirit of the whole group. Millais and the Rossettis were the chief satellites' (letter dated 1 December 1896, folios 110-11, MS.Don.e.81, Bodleian Library, Oxford).

10. JBD, 15 September 1853, p. 47.

11. They were often placed in albums, like the one that belonged to the Wyatt family. See Funnell and Warner 1999, pp. 41-3, 51.

12. Letter dated 1 December 1896 (see note 9).

13. JBD, entry for 18 May 1853, p. 37. Brett's spelling and punctuation are sometimes inaccurate, we have retained them throughout the text.

14. Funnell and Warner 1999, p. 78.

15. Letter dated 1 December 1896, folios 110-11, MS.Don.e.81, Bodleian Library, Oxford.

16. Anstruther 1992.

17. JBD, p. 19.

18. Pettigrew 1981, pp. 819, 1161.

19. JBD, Christmas Day 1852, p. 22.

20. JBD, 5 February 1853, p. 27.

21. See note 2.

22. JBD, 15 February 1853, p. 28,

23. Ibid., 1 December 1852, pp. 20-21.

24. Lloyd and Sloan 2008.

25. Brett's early diary ends abruptly in August 1854, with just a few later entries in December 1856, December 1858, July 1859 and January 1860. For 1857, as in 1855, there are no entries at all.

26. JBD, 9 December 1856, p. 63.

27. Anon (Coventry Patmore), 'A Pre-Raphaelite Exhibition', *Saturday Review*, 4 July 1857, p. 12.

28. The evidence is examined in Marsh 1994, pp. 200-17. See also Hickox 1985, pp. 105-10.

29. For example, in May 1863 the diarist Arthur Munby records that Rossetti described Brett as 'insufferable, ignorant ... a stupid literalist (with) "no more eye for colour than a pig"'. Munby, who was a friend of Brett, was indignant and thought this criticism quite unfair (Hudson 1972, pp. 160-61, entry for 12 May 1863).

30. When a number of Pre-Raphaelite paintings were rejected by the selectors of the Royal Academy exhibition in 1863, Hunt tried to get Brett to coordinate an alternative exhibition at the Cosmopolitan Club. Brett, however, decided to show his two rejected works in his studio instead, a development which aroused Hunt's indignation.

31. The self portrait is now in the Huntington Library and Art Gallery, San Marino, California.

32. JBD, 25 December 1858, p. 64.

33. Letter from John Ruskin to John Brett, 2 May 1863, from Tailloires, Lake of Annecy, private collection.

34. Letter from John Ruskin to Thomas Plint, undated, John Rylands Library, University of Manchester, 1254 letter 15.

35. Letter from John Ruskin (see note 33).

36. Letter from John James Ruskin to John Brett, dated 30 July 1863, private collection.

37. GWD, 8 February 1865, p. 3.

38. Tennyson and Browning both address their lovers as 'my dove' in well-known poems (*Maud* and *Two in the Campagna*); Hawthorne's novel is entitled *The Marble Faun*. If (as seems likely) she was a professional singer, Jeannette might well have sung the hymn *Hear my Prayer*, by Mendelssohn, which contains the celebrated line 'Oh for the wings of a dove'. Artistic associations of women with doves from this period include Millais's painting *My Dove (Miss Siddal)* (1862), a medallion by Alexander Munro, *Eva Butler with a Live Dove* (1864, private collection), and a watercolour by John Frederick Lewis, *Caged Doves, Cairo* (1864, Fitzwilliam Museum, Cambridge).

39. Letters from John Brett to Alfred Morrison, dated 18 July, 27 July and 4 August 1865, Morrison archives, private collection.

40. Letter from John Brett to Alfred Morrison, dated 17 August 1866, Morrison archives, private collection. On the same day Georgina wrote in her diary: 'Brett came at ½ past 10 & began a lovely sketch of me. I went with him to his chambers where Harry [her husband] joined us & we had an oyster luncheon - went to the S. Kensington Museum & then to the National Portrait Gallery wh bored me intensely' (GWD, p. 5).

41. Letter from John Brett to Alfred Morrison, dated 22 August 1866, Morrison archives, private collection.

42. Receipt dated 17 July 1868, Morrison archives, private collection.

43. GWD, 29 August 1866, p. 5.

44. Letter from John Brett to Alfred Morrison, 17 August 1866, Morrison archives, private collection.

45. GWD, 14 June 1868, p. 8: 'Wanted to write Brett a letter which Harry would not let me send he wants me to sit for my portrait and I wont.'

46. For drawings of Ottilie Blind, see Sketchbook no. 30, PAF 9437-9.

47. Letter from John Brett to Alfred Morrison, 7 June 1867, Morrison archives, private collection (fig. 31). The seascape in question was *Christmas Morning, 1866* (Russell-Cotes Museum and Art Gallery, Bournemouth).

48. Mary Ann Howcroft was the daughter of a coachman. In the 1861 census the family are recorded as living in the stables to Lower Woodside House, Hatfield, Herts. William, aged 20, was a helper in the stables; the other children were James (12), George (10) and Eliza (7). The census return for 1851, when they were living at 20 Polygon Mews East, Paddington, records an additional older child Edward (13). In the 1861 census, 'Mary Houghcroft' was a housemaid living at 42 Sloane Square, in the household of Sarah Evans, 'Cow Keeper'.

49. ET, 7 September 1879, p. 2.

50. Edith Simcox, *Autobiography*, 9 March 1880 cited in Haight 1978, vol. ix, p. 298.

51. ET, 2 September 1883, p. 20.

52. ET, 20 August 1882 p. 13.

53. ET, 5 October 1879, p. 4; 1 February 1889, p. 52.

Brett and Birmingham:
'tho' inland far we be, Our souls have sight of that immortal sea'

Ann Sumner

John Brett is renowned for his luminous, atmospheric depictions of unspoilt remote areas of the British coastline. It is somewhat surprising, then, to learn that this Victorian artist had a close relationship with landlocked Birmingham, the industrial powerhouse of Britain in the 19th century.[1] Brett's most beautiful idyllic coastal views adorned the walls of the new homes of Birmingham's manufacturing elite, especially in the favoured Edgbaston area, where the Barber Institute of Fine Arts is situated today. Brett was familiar with the West Midlands from his teenage years when his father, an army veterinary surgeon (no. 19), was stationed at Coventry. Once established as an artist, he exhibited his paintings regularly at the Royal Birmingham Society of Artists (RBSA) in its impressive building on New Street (fig. 15).[2] From 1858 to 1901, he sent 56 works for display, including some of his best-known paintings such as *The Hedger* (1859-60, fig. 16) and *Britannia's Realm* (1880, Tate Britain).[3] The annual exhibitions of watercolours in the spring and oils in the autumn attracted a wide range of artists and over 40,000 visitors. Brett was also encouraged by an early success in Birmingham when the Corporation purchased, in 1873, *North-West Gale off the Longships Lighthouse*, for their future gallery (fig. 19). Later, when the City Museum and Art Gallery opened in 1885, Brett lent *The Isles of Skomer and Skokham* (fig. 26) to a major exhibition of 'living marine painters' in 1894. He was further represented in that exhibition by ten other seascapes. The catalogue described Brett's work thus: 'His sapphire and turquoise blue seas are marvels of draughtsmanship and colour'.[4]

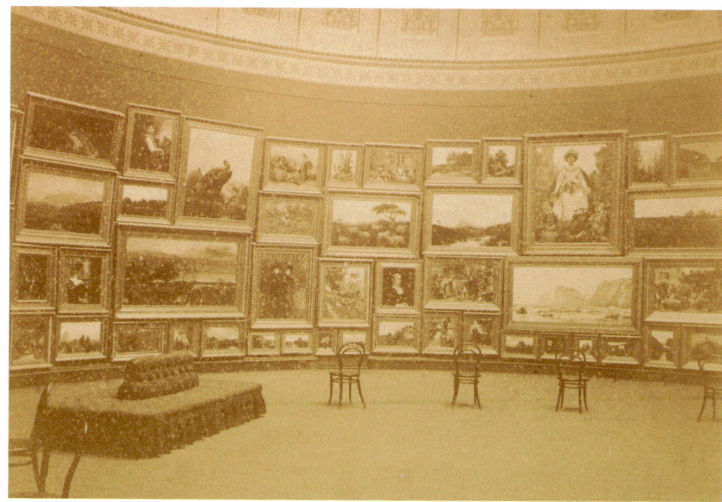

Fig. 15 ***The Viewing Rooms at the Royal Birmingham Society of Artists***
1880s, photograph

By the 1870s Brett had established a working pattern, spending his summer months by the sea, making sketches that would inform a winter of painting. He had already acquired some of his key patrons such as Alfred Morrison (no. 33) by this period. While he did go on to cultivate some aristocratic patrons such as the Duke of Westminster, many of Brett's patrons came from outside London and were self-made industrialists such as Thomas Taylor of Wigan (1810 - 1892), the cotton tycoon, Joseph Ruston of Lincoln (1835 - 1897) who built steam engines, and Alexander Macdonald (1881 - 1834), owner of a granite works at Aberdeen. In Birmingham and the West Midlands though, Brett built up a group of supporters who were linked through business and family connections. Many were industrialists, others were professional men, and a number became friends, whom the artist visited regularly. While Brett was far away by the sea, these patrons in landlocked Birmingham were often on his mind. During the summer of 1882 while on the Welsh coast at Newport in Pembrokeshire he wrote to Thomas Horsfall of Manchester, to whose pioneering Ancoats Museum he had presented a Cornish seascape. He explained that he favoured Birmingham, rather than Manchester, for the regular exhibition of his work.

> *I did once send a picture to the Manchester Royal Institution but they hung it in a very obscure place and scratched it so badly ... I never sent anything since, partly for that reason and partly that no Manchester man ever buys of me. Birmingham men do buy of me and I therefore always try to send them something for their exhibitions.*[5]

Indeed, Brett often went to considerable lengths to accommodate the RBSA. For instance, in 1874, under some pressure, he sent two small oil sketches of Cornish and Welsh scenery to the spring exhibition with the proviso that 'it be distinctly understood that they are mere sketches from nature not retouched afterwards', adding that he would not normally exhibit such works and did so only 'because requested by your deputation'.[6] The experiment was clearly successful as the following year he sent two more Cornish sketches, this time of Bude, to the spring show.[7] The *Birmingham Gazette* reported that they were 'fine vigorous

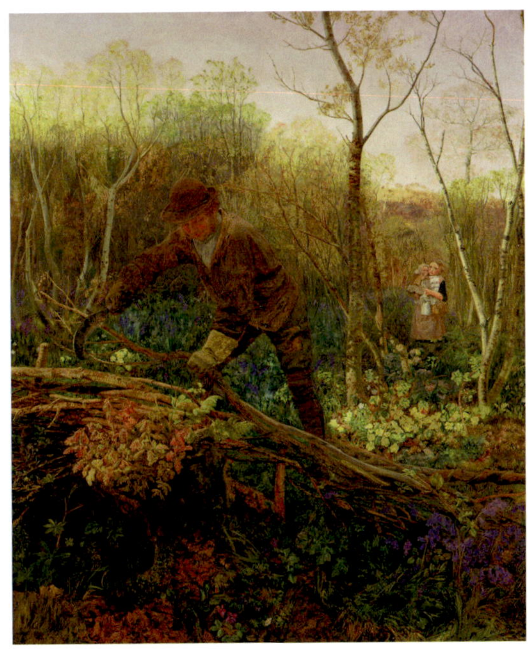

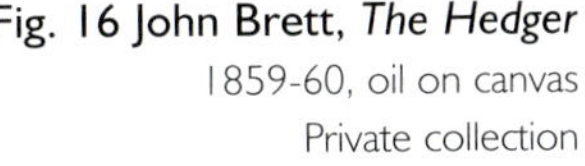

Fig. 16 John Brett, *The Hedger*
1859-60, oil on canvas
Private collection

sketches of rolling seas and toppling masses of cloud, showing the artist to greater advantage than many of his more finished works.'[8] In July 1881 he wrote from Cornwall to the Society to explain that he could not borrow back his Academy piece that year for their show but added 'I am therefore painting a picture express for that purpose'.[9] The work would be ready by early August. However, he did express concern about who would pay the transport from Cornwall to Birmingham! This work was *The Wind Offshore: Towan Head, Cornwall* (untraced) and was exhibited in the autumn show.[10] In contrast to his thoughts on the hanging of his work in Manchester, he approved of the display of his pictures in Birmingham, where he dealt with the honorary curator/secretary Jonathan Pratt (1835 - 1911). When passing through Birmingham in 1888 Brett noted, 'I saw my chief academy picture of last year [*The Earth's Shadow on the Sky*] at the R Society of Artists. It had the centre in the long room and looked very well' (fig. 24).[11]

No sketches of Birmingham itself survive by Brett, although early on in his career he had an extended stay in the West Midlands, sketching and working up a view of *Warwick Castle* (fig. 17, finished work untraced) in July 1860.[12] He stayed in the area from June to December and was joined for a while by his sister Rosa (no. 23) and later by Fanny Bell as well (no. 22). Brett and his sister took the opportunity to catch up with some old friends in the area, the Salters at Leamington, and the Craggs at Coventry. By the 1870s, with his reputation as a painter of the sea growing, Brett was firmly established with a circle of prominent Birmingham patrons. He wrote from Weymouth on the Dorset coast to his brother Arthur (no. 2), a lieutenant in the army, during the summer of 1874: 'My RA picture Summer noon in the Scilly Isles was sold, as I probably told you, in my studio for £500 to an old acquaintance Martin of Birmingham ... Spent a week at Birmingham with Martin and met some of the hardware people who go in for pictures.'[13] William Martin (1829 - 1900) of Bournbrook Hall in Stirchley, was a prominent Birmingham architect, designer of many public works, and a very well-connected friend to have made. Brett invested the £500 swiftly in 'Great Western of Canada Debentures' in order that 'the chicks should have something in case I get snuffed out'.[14]

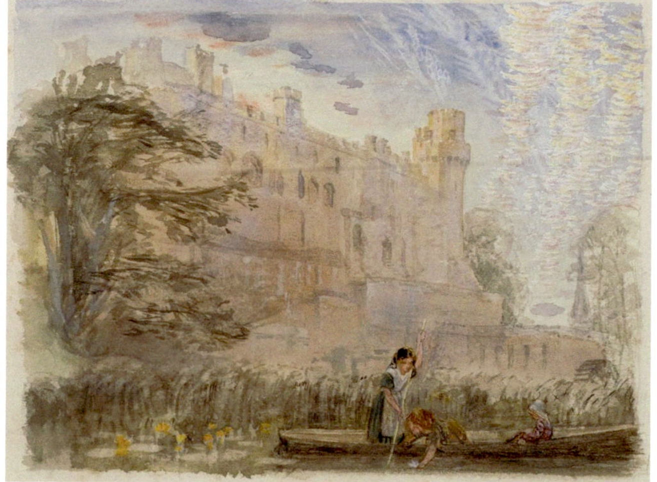

Fig. 17 John Brett, *Study for Warwick Castle*
1860, watercolour on paper
Private collection

Martin's many business links throughout the city enormously benefited Brett's career. He was himself an enthusiastic patron, buying his first work by Brett, *November in the Isle of Wight*, in 1865 for £75 (untraced), followed by *February in the Isle of Wight* of 1866 (fig. 18) for £45.[15] Both watercolours were exhibited at the RBSA in their spring show. Martin went on to buy the aforementioned *Summer Noon in the Scilly Isles* for £500 and *Sir Thomas's Tower* (both untraced) of 1876. He owned two further seascapes of 1876 and 1894, the latter being presented to him as a gift. In that same year Martin patronised Brett's daughter Daisy, an aspiring young artist, paying £15 for one of her pictures.

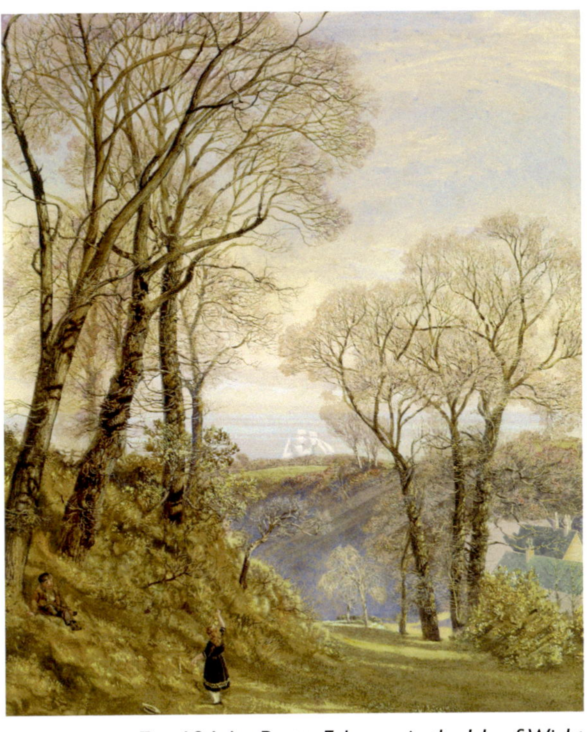

Fig. 18 John Brett, *February in the Isle of Wight*
1866, watercolour on paper
Birmingham Museums & Art Gallery

It was through Martin that Brett was introduced to his partner, John Henry Chamberlain (1831 - 1883), an architect of remarkable talent who designed, amongst other buildings, the Oozells Street Board School, now the Ikon Gallery, in Brindley Place, the Birmingham School of Art in Margaret Street and houses such as The Grove, Harborne, for William Kenrick and Highbury Hall, for Joseph Chamberlain. Both J. H. Chamberlain and Kenrick were trustees of the Birmingham Public Picture Gallery Fund and may have been responsible for influencing the decision to purchase *A North-West Gale off the Longships Lighthouse* (fig. 19) in 1873 for 400 gns, after it was shown at the RBSA having failed to sell at the RA in the spring. This commanding, large-scale work was destined for a new public art gallery for Birmingham and was the first of his paintings to be publicly purchased.[16] It was exhibited initially at the Royal Academy as a pair with *A Morning Amongst the Granite Boulders* (fig. 20). The impressive seven-foot-wide paintings showed the impact of a storm and its aftermath and both attracted favourable reviews. The latter work also came to Birmingham, entering the collection of David Hodges of Yardley, a subscriber to the RBSA, although it was not exhibited there.[17] He acquired it after it was lent to the City Art Gallery's show of marine painters in 1894. However, later large works sent to Birmingham did not tend to sell so well. It was essentially a market for paintings on a domestic scale that Brett had nurtured in the West Midlands.

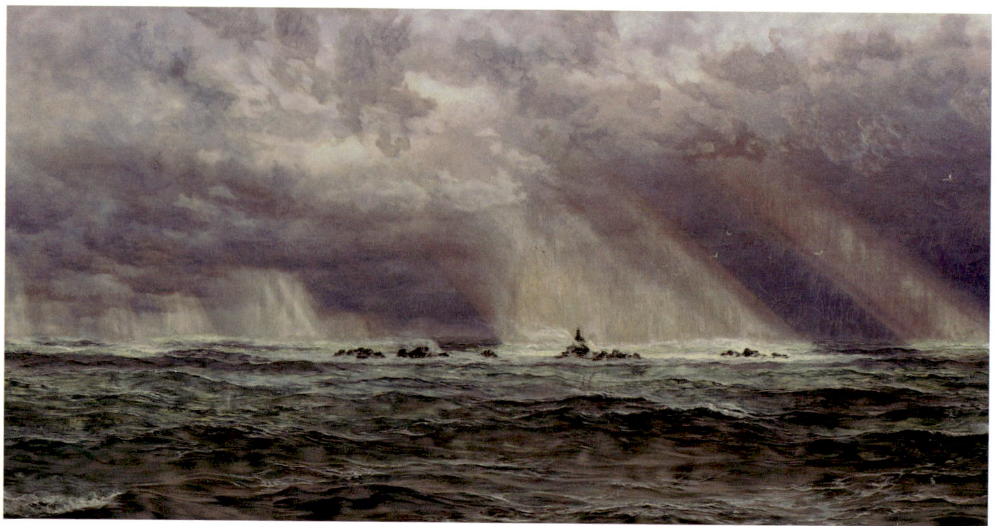

Fig. 19 John Brett, *A North-West Gale off the Longships Lighthouse*
1873, oil on canvas
Birmingham Museums & Art Gallery

The high standards of craftsmanship and design of Martin and Chamberlain's architectural partnership encouraged Brett to use them himself to build the new home he was planning in 1877 at 6 Keswick Road, Putney. Although living in London, he also employed the builders John Barnsley & Sons of Ryland Street in Birmingham. Brett was fascinated by architecture and was delighted with their work. There appears to have been real friendship and mutual admiration between Brett and Martin, especially when a legal case with the Guildford and Kingston railway, relating to the later compulsory purchase of 6 Keswick Road, dragged on. Brett reported that the matter 'has at length been closed ... our dear old friend, William Martin of Birmingham was the chief figure in this long contest and the chief agent in our success. He was the arbitrator and his skill in drawing the agreement under which the arbitration was applied was incomparable.'[18]

Brett was equally fond of J. H. Chamberlain who was living at Grange House, Small Heath when Brett first met him. When Chamberlain unexpectedly died in 1883, the artist was a pall-bearer at his funeral.[19] The architect was impressed by Brett's landscapes and purchased two oil sketches, *Caernarvon* of October 1875 and *Kennack Sands* in Cornwall of August 1876 (nos. 40 and 42). In early 1879, at a time when Chamberlain was building himself a new house, Whetstone, in Edgbaston, Brett borrowed back the *Caernarvon* sketch, to assist him in painting a large work for exhibition at the Royal Academy. That painting, *The Stronghold of the Seison* (fig. 22), failed to sell later at the RA or at the RBSA where he sent it that autumn.[20] Brett wrote to thank Chamberlain, in February 1879, for the loan, commenting that he was particularly eager to see his new home, 'I have seldom felt so much curiosity as to that new house of yours'.[21] Chamberlain moved in during September and later adorned the house with a further four landscapes by Brett. The artist seems to have borrowed back *Kennack Sands* as well, for in 1883 it appears to have been the inspiration for his Royal Academy painting *These Yellow Sands* (untraced) that year.[22]

Joseph Chamberlain (1836 - 1914), the politician, was not related to J. H. Chamberlain, but was also a patron of Brett in the 1870s. He was appointed first mayor of Birmingham in 1873 thereafter achieving three successive years of office and then entering Parliament in 1876, becoming Secretary of State for the Colonies. He lived initially at Southbourne, Edgbaston where he displayed *In the Channel Islands* of 1876 (untraced), which he already owned when it was exhibited at the RBSA that year.[23] In the last years of his life he retired to the house J. H. Chamberlain had built for him.

The walls of the homes of the Birmingham elite in Edgbaston and the surrounding area were indeed hung with Brett's works - sparkling views of the blue sea of the British coast - views too of Wales (where he hoped to establish a colony for his circle), Cornwall and the Isles of Scilly. Scottish views also proved popular with Birmingham patrons. The banker Joseph Beattie, a subscriber to the RBSA, who lived on the Hagley Road owned two Guernsey views of the 1870s, lending one, *Fermain Bay*, to the Society for their 1875 show.[24] This was described by the *Birmingham Gazette* as 'one of the gems of the exhibition ... one of those wonderful studies of sun-lit rock and bright sea that seem impossible to any other painter,

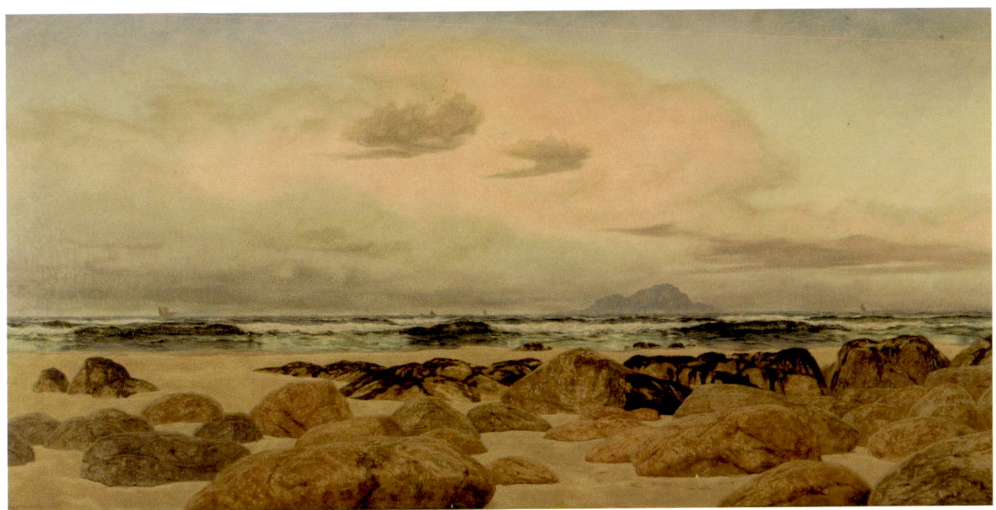

Fig. 20 John Brett, *A Morning Amongst the Granite Boulders*
1873, oil on canvas
Private collection

Fig. 22 John Brett, *Caernarvon (no. 40)*
1875, oil on canvas
Birmingham Museums & Art Gallery

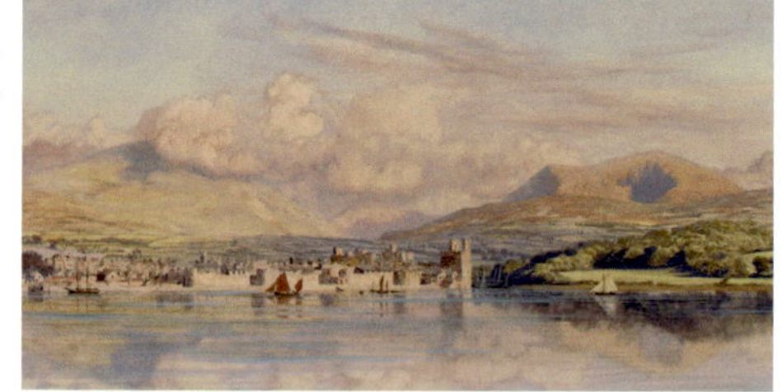

Fig. 21 John Brett, *The Stronghold of the Seison and the Camp of the Kittywake*
1879, oil on canvas
National Museum of Wales, Cardiff

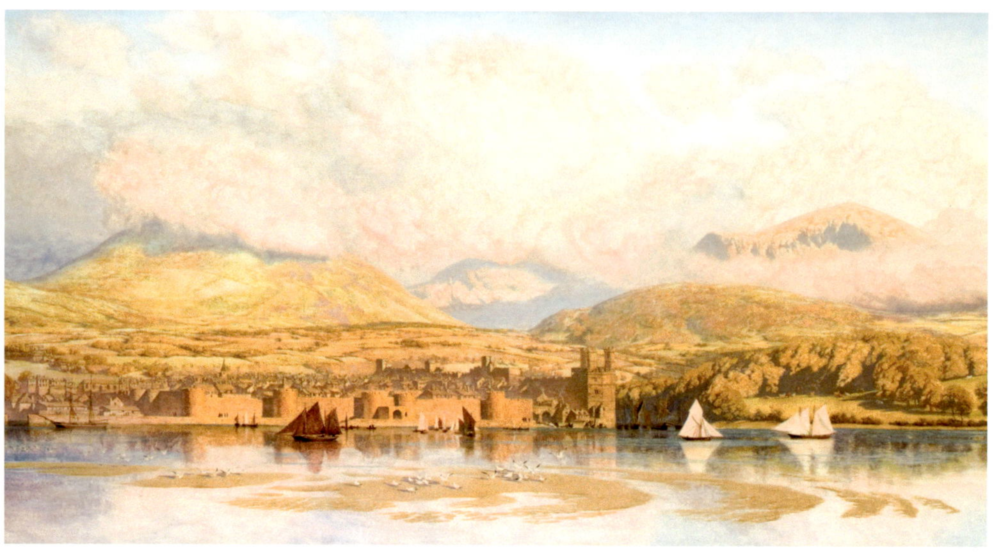

and yet which are achievements easy to Mr Brett: the very look of it sets one longing for a holiday, in such a scene, and under such a sky'.[25] Glass manufacturer Abraham Follett Osler, another subscriber to the RBSA, whose family business was renowned for cut-glass chandeliers and the monumental fountain for the Great Exhibition of 1851, also lent the very fine *Southern Coast of Guernsey* (no. 41) to the Society in 1875. His relation, Alfred Osler of South Bank, Edgbaston, owned a Scottish view, *Loch Baretal*, of 1883.[27] W. H. Smith, another subscriber to the Society, of Ryland Road, Edgbaston, commissioned the distinctive *Cym-yr-Eglas* - a view on the Dinas Island peninsula in Pembrokeshire in 1882, paying £150 for the vibrant work (fig. 23).[28] The building contractor Thomas Barnsley, whose family business built Brett's Putney homes, lived at Augustus Road and then Southerndown, Edgbaston and became a late patron owning *Sea Mists, Cardigan Bay* of 1892 (untraced) and going on to purchase three more Bretts. Slightly further afield, Alderman Ambrose Briggs of Groveley, Northfield Station, owned two views of Betws-y-Coed (1875), a location made popular in Birmingham by David Cox. The brewer Sir John Holder of Moor Green also owned another Scottish view *An Argyll Eden* of 1886.[29]

Joseph Chamberlain was the brother-in-law of William Kenrick (1831 - 1919), an iron founder and hardware manufacturer. Kenrick, a Unitarian, had married Mary Chamberlain in 1862. He was MP for Birmingham North and mayor in 1877. Not only was he a trustee of the Public Picture Gallery Fund, but also chairman of the Museum and School of Arts Committee and became a director of the Birmingham Guild of Handicraft when it became a limited company in 1895. Kenrick was a key patron of the arts and favoured Brett, displaying such works as *A Summer Day, South Wales, White Sands Bay*, 1872 (no. 39) for which he paid £150 and *The South Bishop Rock; Anticipations of a Wild Night* (private collection) in his new impressive Chamberlain-designed house The Grove, Park Lane, Harborne (now demolished). A friend of Sir Edward Burne Jones (1838 - 1898), Kenrick also acquired two smaller works by Brett and a fine Henry Moore (1831 - 1895) seascape.[30] Altogether, around thirty Bretts were owned in the fashionable southern suburbs of Birmingham.

Birmingham and West Midlands industrial patrons had helped make Brett a rich and successful artist but there was a distinct falling off in his sales throughout the late 1880s and 90s. Although Brett had admired the way that *The Earth's Shadow on the Sky* (fig. 24) had been displayed at the RBSA in 1888, he had also observed that it remained unsold. 'No-one has attempted to buy it and things look like starvation at home'.[31] He may, however, simply have overpriced it at £1,000.[32] This lack of sales, which continued into the 1890s, reflected a shift in taste amongst the public and critics alike towards French Impressionist art. Some patrons, such as Sir Alfred Hickman, ironmaster and the Wolverhampton MP, and the builder Barnsley, remained loyal into the 1890s, although the former drove a hard bargain with the

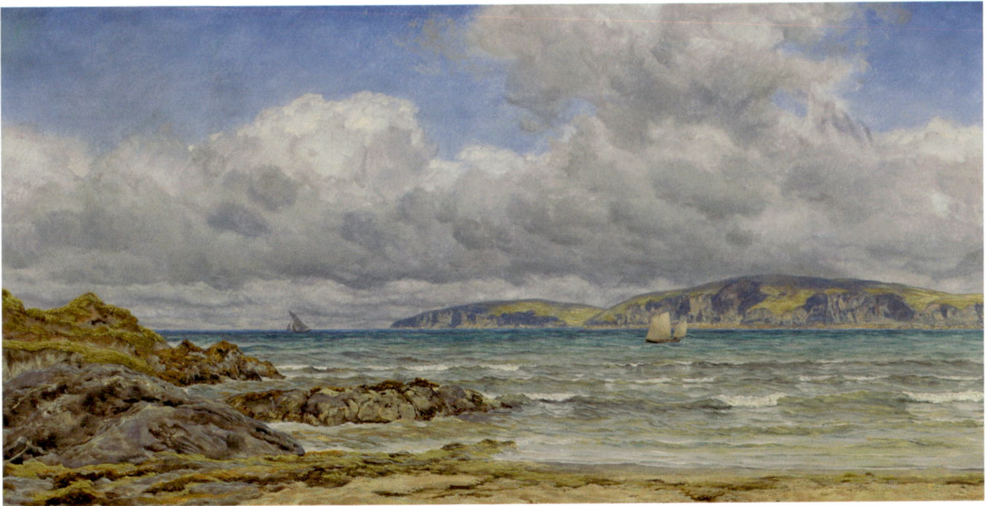

Fig. 23 John Brett, *Cym-yr-Eglas*
1882, oil on canvas
Private collection

last works that he purchased from Brett, two views of Putney Heath exhibited at the Royal Academy and originally priced at £150. Brett was eventually grateful to accept £75.[33] Other patrons turned elsewhere altogether. The RBSA was also seeing a reduction in attendance, as it faced competition from the new City Art Gallery. Gradually a decline in Brett's sales resulted in a reduction in income leading to financial woes, especially as he had such a large family and an expensive lifestyle which included owning a yacht and paying public school fees.

With the compensation funds gained from the forced sale of his house in Putney, Brett amused himself designing and building a new home, Daisyfield, on the land he purchased in 1887 at Putney Heath. Despite his concern over finances, the new house went ahead with Brett overseeing the innovative open-plan design. When Beatrix Potter visited she commented, 'His house is a curiosity, planned by himself, all on one floor, in the ecclesiastical cruciform, without fireplace or originally doors, but it was so uncomfortable that they added some'.[34] What is extraordinary about Daisyfield is that despite being built in London, Brett again employed Birmingham firms to carry out many aspects of the work. Martin was once again the architect, John Barnsley & Sons, the builders, with Cotterill & Co providing the locks, William Tonks & Sons supplying the brass fittings, George Hadley of Edgbaston produced the gas pipes, and even the wire for the garden fence came from Bayliss, Jones & Bayliss of Wolverhampton.[35] Given the logistical difficulties of transportation and Brett's difficult financial position, it seems probable that he used his Martin connections to get good prices from these firms. When the house was finally finished Brett presented Martin with a painting, *July*, as a present on 'concluding the business of Daisyfield'.[36]

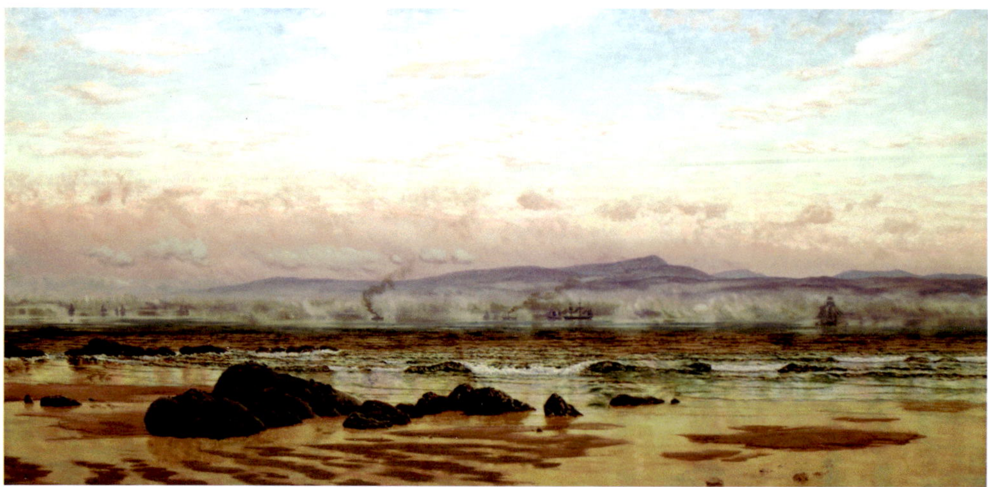

Fig. 24 John Brett, *The Earth's Shadow on the Sky*
1888, oil on canvas
Sunderland Museum and Winter Gardens

Lecturing and writing increasingly appealed to Brett, whose health was declining by the late 1880s, and here too Birmingham played a role. During the summer of 1890 Brett and the family travelled to Scotland and stayed at the shooting lodge at Kylestrome belonging to his patron the Duke of Westminster, and which was offered to the family in payment for a picture.[37] He had come to paint, but found it 'hopelessly difficult'. Instead, he concentrated on writing his lecture for the National Association for the Advancement of Art and its Application to Industry for their Birmingham meeting that November.[38] In Scotland he was able to vent his frustrations, looking out on 'one of the loveliest scenes in the Highlands - the Glendhu', covered by 'veils of mist that characterise the Scotch climate'. The original manuscript, much annotated, survives (fig. 25).[39]

Brett was in Birmingham by late October and stayed until the 8th of November. 'My Birmingham paper would be quite useless for boys,' he explained to a friend. 'It is not even addressed to the Birmingham public, except nominally. It is really addressed to the supposed authorities on the subject, and the impudently self-appointed critics.'[40] In the lecture, Brett explained that he would 'deal chiefly with the education of the professional painter and sculptor, but I shall also have something to say as to the artistic education of the public'.[41] He defended the Royal Academy system of training, but damned the fashion of English and American students currently entering French studios as pupils. He abhorred the fact that England was now flooded with sham Corots of a miserably low standard.[42] Brett praised J. D. Harding as a draughtsman over Constable, whom he felt 'never could draw'. Other artists of whom he was critical included the Dutch 17th-century master Van de Velde who 'had evidently never seen any water that was not opaque with mud', and Turner whose seas were 'utterly and completely wrong'. Finally, he felt that the French artist Millet's works were worthless and would be entirely forgotten in four years.[43]

Drawing, Brett believed, was best learnt initially by studying the nude, and he lamented the lack of contemporary inspirational landscape artists and sea painters. Despite his pessimism, he felt that young artists were working with 'eagerness and honesty'. *The Times* reported the next day, on the 6th of November, that 'the discussion which ensued, though generally complimentary to the lecturer, disclosed the presence of several strong dissenters'.[44] In fact, when the lecture was published in 1891 that assessment seemed an understatement. The artist Alfred East (1844 - 1913) passionately defended Constable and Stanhope Forbes (1857 - 1947), who was about to deliver the next paper, suggested 'Brett must be mistaken in his assessment of Millet', sarcastically noting that he was delighted 'to think that in four years he should be able to acquire the masterpieces of Millet to put on his walls'.[45] Some of the most stinging comments came from George Whitworth Wallis (1811 - 1891), who was the first director of Birmingham City Art Gallery.[46] He thought that 'some of Mr Brett's statements did not do very great credit to his judgement. He spoke in a ridiculous manner about ... Van de Velde'. Brett defended himself robustly, saying that he admired Van de Velde, but felt the way that the artist painted water was like 'stone' and affirmed his opinion that Millet 'could not draw, and never could'.[47] The reception of his paper must have meant it was a gruelling experience for Brett, but it does not seem to have done his reputation in the city long-term damage. When the City Art Gallery mounted its exhibition of marine paintings four years later, it was one of Brett's large paintings, the dramatic *The Isles of Skomer and Skokham* (fig. 26), which was the first on view in the Long Gallery.

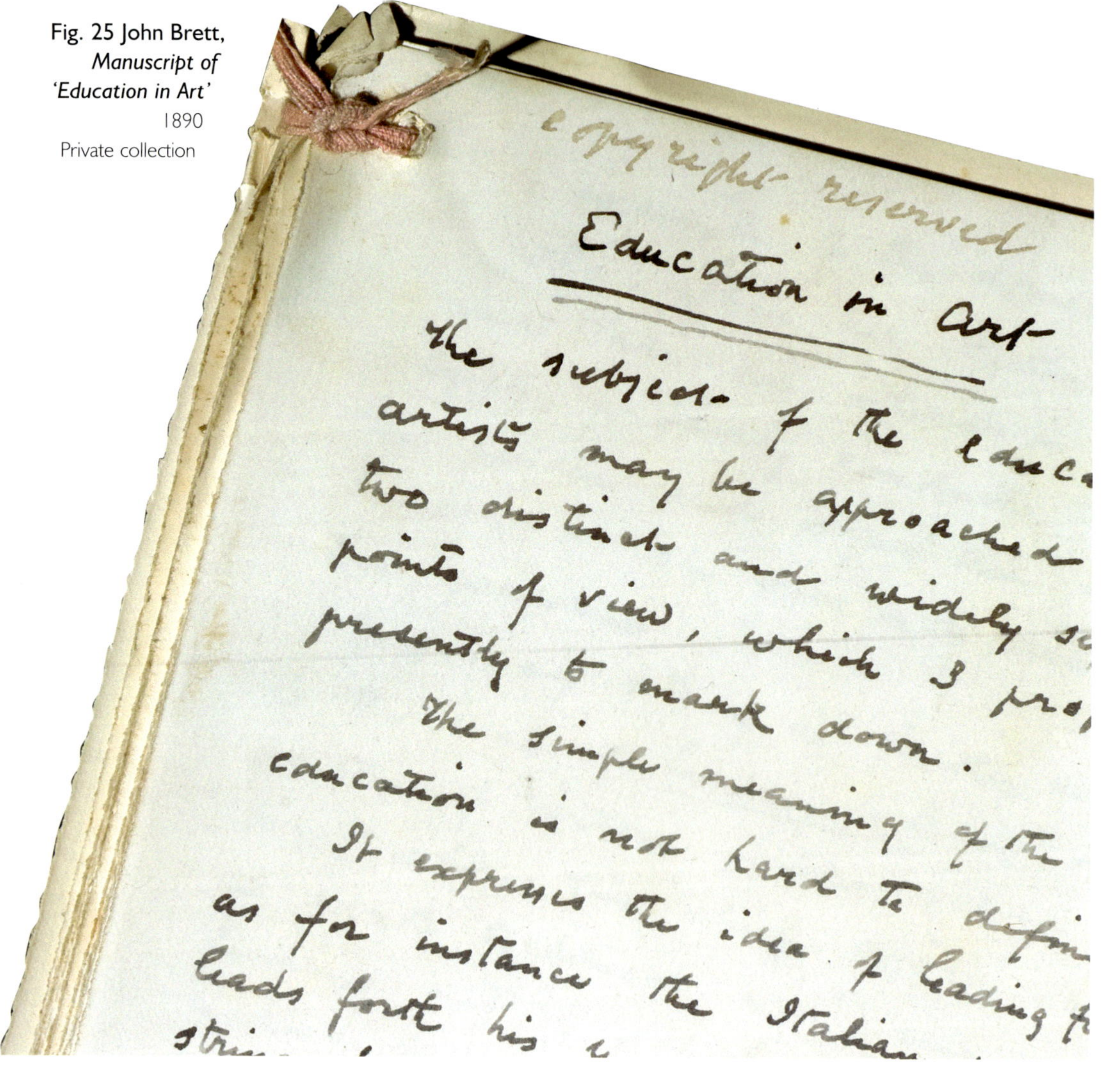

copyright reserved

Education in Art

The subject of the educa
artists may be approached
two distinct and widely se
points of view, which I pro
presently to mark down.
The simple meaning of the
education is not hard to defin
It expresses the idea of leading f
as for instance the Italian
leads forth his

Fig. 25 John Brett, *Manuscript of 'Education in Art'* 1890 Private collection

After Brett's death there was a continued decline in interest in his work. When a revival did occur in the 1970s, led by Allen Staley, there was a concentration upon his early Pre-Raphaelite period.[48] For many years, the output of Brett's later career as a painter of seascapes remained, as Stephen Wildman put it in 1995, 'an important but sadly neglected body of work'.[49] Recent exhibitions in Cardiff (2001) and Penzance (2006) and Christiana Payne's new book, *John Brett Pre-Raphaelite Landscape Painter* (2010) have sought to redress that balance. Sadly, Birmingham no longer boasts the great number of Brett's sea pictures that were here in the 19th century. Later generations who inherited such works found them unfashionable and they were sold. A few made their way into the City Art Gallery. One was left by a descendant of the glass maker Abraham Osler to the University of Birmingham in 1927, but this was presented to the City Art Gallery as the Barber Institute had not yet been founded. It was not until the Barber accepted in 2007, on long-term loan from the Andrew Brownsword Arts Foundation, *The River Dart* (no. 38), that Brett's work went on public view in Edgbaston, finally reflecting the fact that his greatest admirers and patrons had displayed his seascapes in this leafy suburb. *The River Dart* had belonged to Alfred Morrison whose portrait Brett did draw and which is included in the current exhibition (no. 33). Sadly, no portraits of his Birmingham patrons are recorded, and it is unlikely that he made any. This group of wealthy men were, however, an enormous influence on his career and the fashion for his works in Edgbaston and southern Birmingham is celebrated for the first time with this exhibition. The Barber Institute marks the occasion with the acquisition of a small oil sketch *Kennack Sands* (no. 42), which once belonged to J. H. Chamberlain.

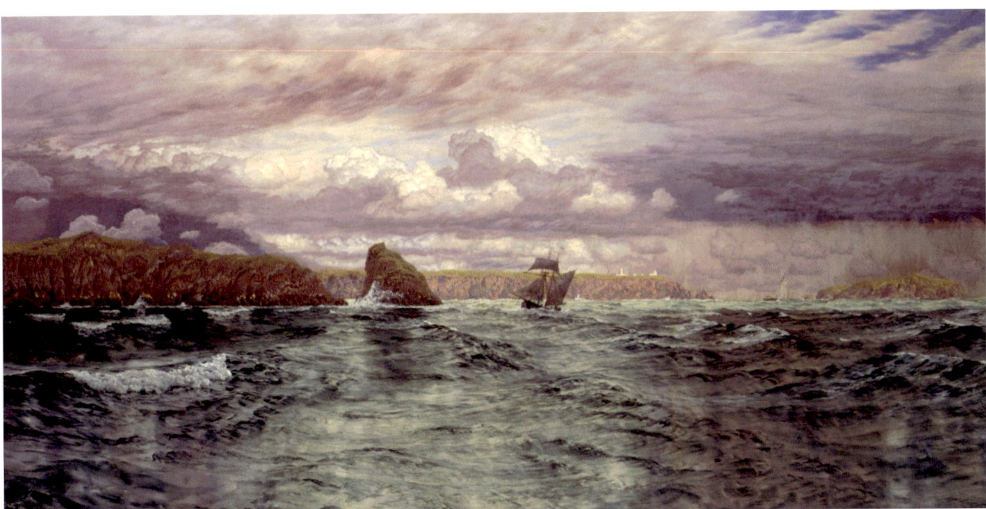

Fig. 26 John Brett, *The Isles of Skomer and Skokham*
1891, oil on canvas
Aberdeen Art Gallery and Museum

Notes

1. Birmingham's landlocked status was recognised by the quote used from William Wordsworth's ode, *Intimations of Immortality*, which was used as the prefix of the exhibition of *Marine Painters* organised by the City of Birmingham Museum and Art Gallery in 1894. Brett's works featured so prominently in the show. The same quotation forms part of the title to this essay.

2. Founded in 1842, and originally known as the Society of Artists, Birmingham, it is now known as the Royal Birmingham Society of Artists (RBSA). The Society is based in Brook Street, the original Thomas Rickman building having been demolished. A petition for patronage was granted by Queen Victoria in 1868 allowing the Society the prefix 'Royal'.

3. RBSA, 1865, no. 52 as 'The Property of B G Windus'. The Tottenham builder and pill manufacturer had a celebrated art collection, including works by Millais, Madox Brown, Hunt and Hughes (Brett 2004, p. 4). RBSA, Autumn Exhibition, 1880, no. 408 as 'The Property of the Royal Academy'.

4. Marine Painters 1894, p. 10.

5. John Brett to T. C. Horsfall, 11 July 1882, Horsfall Papers, Manchester City Art Gallery. In fact, Brett exhibited at Manchester on a number of occasions, including *Lady with a Dove* (no. 3).

6. John Brett to the RBSA, 12 February 1874, Archives of the RBSA. The works sent were RBSA, Spring Exhibition, no. 639 *At St Ives* and no. 651 *Sketch at Aberamffra*.

7. RBSA, Spring Exhibition, 1875, nos. 447 and 460.

8. *Birmingham Gazette*, 19 April 1875, Press Cuttings Book, Archives of the RBSA.

9. John Brett to Mr Everitt at the RBSA, 23 July 1881, Archives of the RBSA.

10. RBSA, Autumn Exhibition, 1881, no. 426.

11. SL, 10 December 1888. The work, shown in the RBSA Autumn Exhibition (no. 81), was eventually acquired by Sunderland Museum and Art Gallery in 1901.

12. The finished picture, known only from an early sketch and a watercolour, was not well reviewed at the Royal Academy but sold to the Leeds stockbroker Thomas Plint (1823 - 1861) for a high price of £420 in January 1861. Brett stayed for ten weeks at Park Cottage for ten shillings a week and then moved to Old Milverton.

13. John Brett to Arthur Brett, 6 July 1874, untraced.

14. Payne 2010, forthcoming.

15. RBSA, Spring Exhibition, 1866, nos. 53 and 87.

16. Brett 2004, p. 9.

17. Brett's larger landscapes appealed to the newly emerging civic galleries. The Public Picture Gallery Fund for Birmingham was established with a gift of £3,000 from Thomas Clarkson Osler, the glass manufacturer whose son patronised Brett. For further information about the Fund and the foundation of Birmingham City Museum and Art Gallery, see Davies 1985, p. 17.

18. ET, 12 September 1886.

19. Hartnell 1996, p. 76. Joseph Chamberlain and William Kenrick were also pall-bearers.

20. Cardiff 2001, no. 15. RBSA, Autumn Exhibition, 1879, no. 78; Royal Academy, London, 1879, no. 643.

21. John Brett to J. H. Chamberlain, 26 February 1879, private collection. I am grateful to Charles Brett for drawing my attention to this letter.

22. SL, 1883 'painted from the sketch at Kennack bought by J H Chamberlain'.

23. RBSA, Autumn Exhibition, 1876, no. 111.

24. RBSA, Autumn Exhibition, 1875, no. 127.

25. *Birmingham Gazette*, 26 August 1875, Press Cuttings Book, Archives of the RBSA.

26. RBSA, Autumn Exhibition, 1875, no. 361.

27. SL, June 1884.

28. RBSA, Autumn Exhibition, 1883, no. 108. See Cardiff 2001, no. 24.

29. RBSA, Autumn Exhibition, 1886, no. 445.

30. Cardiff 2001, no. 7.

31. SL, 10 December 1888.

32. RBSA, Autumn Exhibition, 1888, no. 81.

33. Brett 2004, p. 14.

34. Linder 1966, p. 372, 6 April 1895.

35. Many of the companies' names appear in John Brett's address book (private collection); the reference to Bayliss, Jones & Bayliss is in ET, 12 May 1887.

36. SL, 30 August 1894.

37. Payne 2010, forthcoming.

38. Transactions 1891, p. 122.

39. Private collection, Cambridge.

40. John Brett to Mrs Style, 27 October 1890, Brett family papers. I am grateful to Charles Brett for drawing my attention to this letter.

41. Transactions 1891, p. 111.

42. Ibid., p. 117.

43. Ibid., p. 118. He did not specify which Van de Velde.

44. *The Times*, 6 November 1890, p. 10.

45. Stanhope Forbes was to lecture on 'The Treatment of Modern Life in Art' (Transactions 1891, p. 123).

46. For more information on George Whitworth Wallis, see Davies 1985, p. 26.

47. Transactions 1891, p. 123.

48. Staley 1973, pp. 124-7.

49. Wildman 1995, p. 296.

Opposite Page
Jeannette Loeser in Profile, no. 26
1863, pencil on paper
Private collection

Catalogue

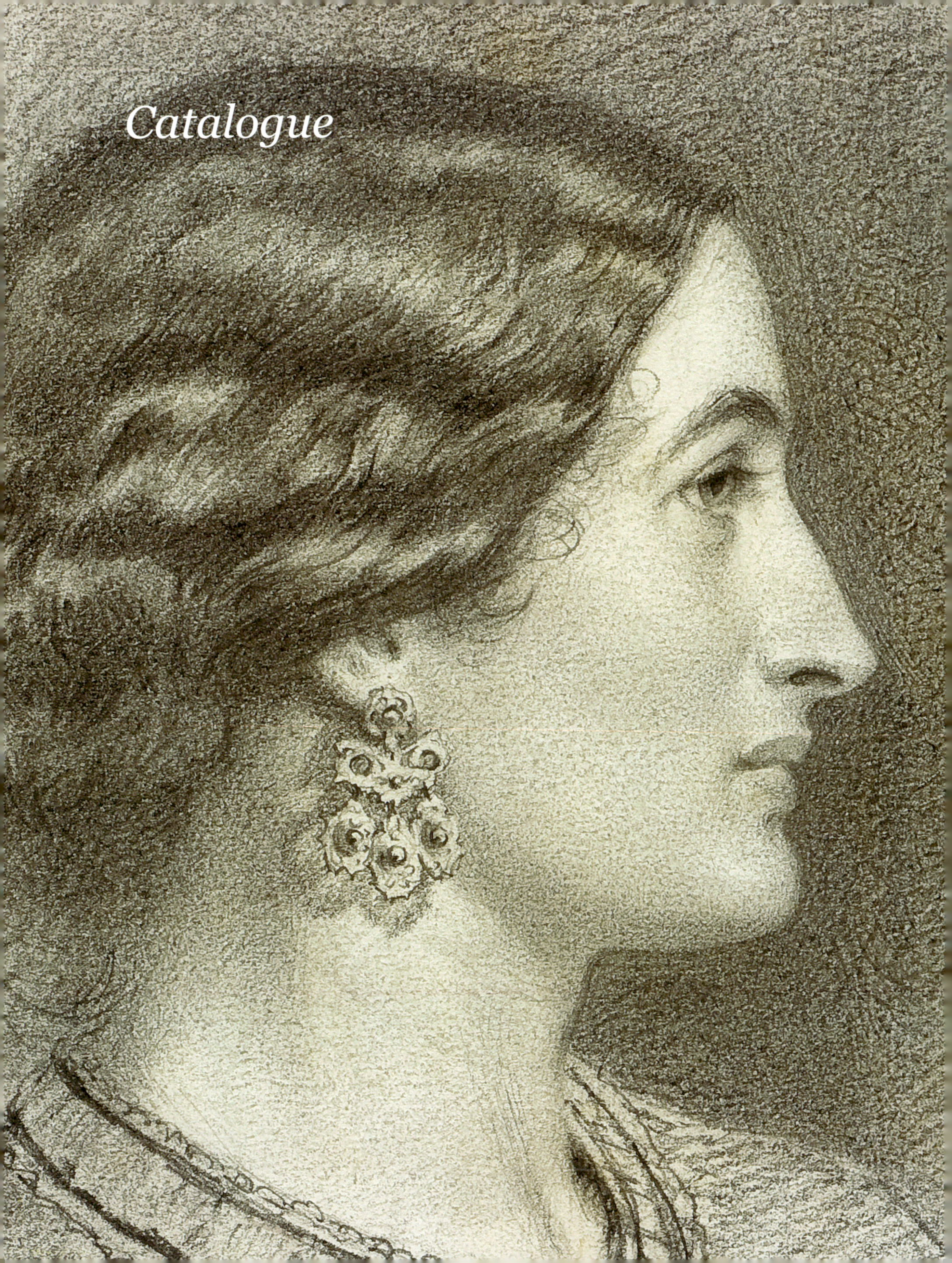

Portraits in Oils

1 *Christina Rossetti* (1857)
Oil on panel
13.3 x 10.1 cms.
Inscribed: 'Christina Rossetti (?) Mickleham 1857'
(on reverse, probably by Winifred Watson, Brett's granddaughter)
Private collection

The inscription on this unfinished portrait is not in Brett's own hand, but that of his granddaughter. Nevertheless, there seems no reason to challenge the identification and date. In her biography of the poet, Jan Marsh has examined the evidence for a relationship between Christina Rossetti (1830 - 1894) and John Brett, and concludes that Christina's poem, *No, thank you, John*, written in 1860, refers to a courtship which was not entirely unwelcome to her. She further suggests that the period from summer 1857 to summer 1858 is the most likely period for this to have culminated in a proposal which was rejected (Marsh 1994, pp. 200-17, Hickox 1985). In the summer of 1857 Brett was staying at Mickleham and painting the *Stonebreaker* (fig.1). In November of that year Christina wrote a poem about love, *A Birthday*, in which she compares her heart to a singing bird. The feather in Brett's painting could refer to this, or, as Marsh suggests, to her profession as a writer (as the shaft of a quill pen). Alternatively, Brett may have used the conceit to show off his skill in the kind of detailed naturalism achieved by Dürer and recommended by John Ruskin. The portrait is worked like a miniature, on a white ground, with lavish use of ultramarine in the background. Its unfinished state implies that the relationship ended before it could be completed. CP

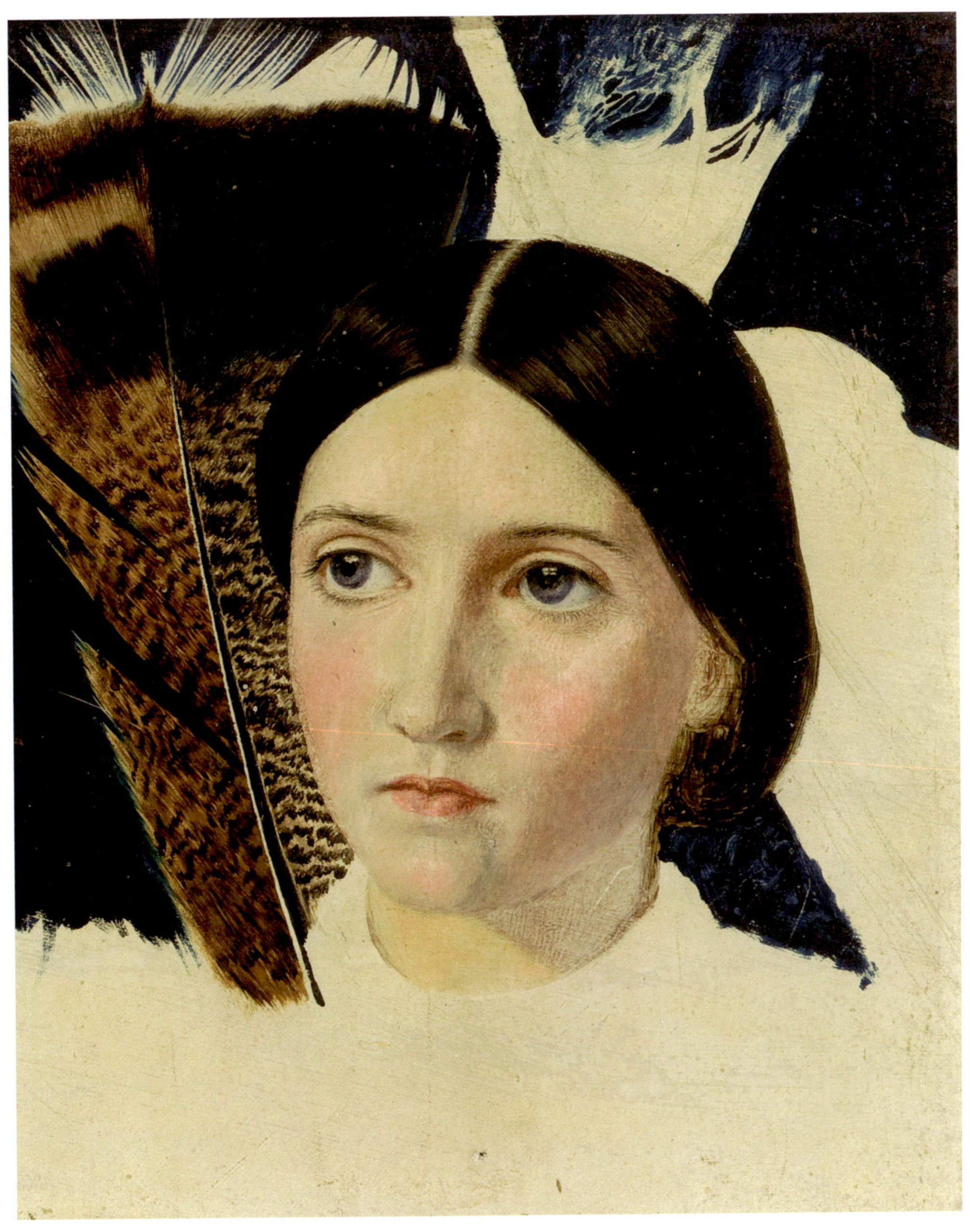

2 ***Arthur Brett*** **(1859)**

Oil on canvas

49 x 41 cms.

Inscribed: 'Portrait of Arthur / John Brett / March 1859' l.l. and 'Lt Colonel Arthur Brett as a young man Queen Bays ... painted by his brother John Brett ara' on reverse

Private collection

This portrait of Brett's brother Arthur (1838 - 1898) was painted in the late winter and early spring of 1859, when Brett declared that he had 'no concern at present but to work for its own sake' (JBD, 25 December 1858, p. 64). Arthur shared lodgings with Brett in London in 1853 and 1854, when he was studying music and hoping to have a career as a pianist, but by 1858 it had been decided that he would enter the army instead. Brett commented on Christmas Day 1858 that 'the sound of his exquisite and wonderful music is just the most melancholy thing in the hemisphere to us now', as Arthur would soon be far from home (ibid.). However, Brett's choice of background, a piece of fabric decorated with lions *passant guardant*, an allusion to the Royal Arms of England, suggests that he had in mind the heroic deeds and chivalrous nature of Arthur's namesake, King Arthur, recently celebrated in Tennyson's *Idylls of the King*. From this more positive standpoint, Brett wrote in his diary: 'I long to see him a real knight seeking adventures the other side of the world, to see all his dreams realized: I would think it enough pleasure for a life … to help the bringing about of them and eyes to see it' (ibid.). As in the drawing of his brother Edwin (no. 14), Arthur gazes directly at the viewer, his piercing stare suggesting courage and integrity, the qualities of a 'real knight'. CP

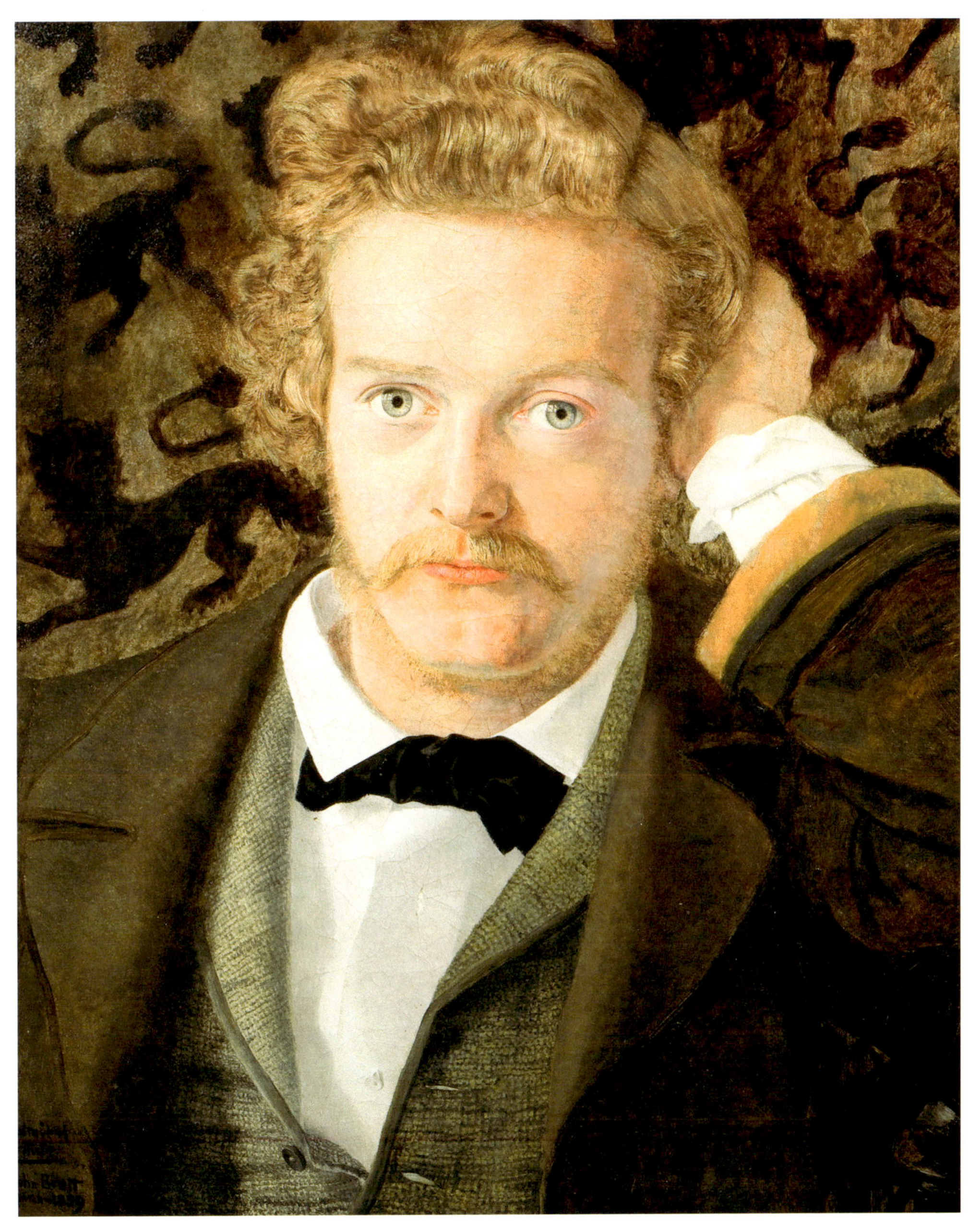

3 *Lady with a Dove (Jeannette Loeser)* (1864)

Oil on canvas
61 x 46 cms.
Inscribed: 'John Brett Aug 1864' l.l.
Exhibited: Royal Manchester Institution, 1865, no. 212 (as *My Dove*)
Tate. Presented by Lady Holroyd in accordance with the wishes of the late Sir Charles Holroyd 1919

Charles Brett's research has proved conclusively that the sitter for this portrait was Jeannette Loeser, companion to the pianist Jacques Blumenthal. The 1851 census records the two lodging together in London, and she evidently took on a maternal role for the pianist. Loeser is variously described as his aunt or his cousin. Both came from Germany. Jacques was born Jacob, but changed his name, probably feeling that a French name would better suit a musical career, and Jeannette may have done the same. In 1851 she was 32, he was 21, and she was described as an 'annuitant': in other words she had a private income so did not need to work, or to marry. When Brett met her in Florence in 1863, she was 44, while he was only 31. Nevertheless, much circumstantial evidence suggests that he became infatuated with her, drawing her repeatedly, and he spent the winters of 1863/4 and 1864/5 with her and Blumenthal on the island of Capri. In the second winter they were joined by Georgina Weldon, whose diary paints a vivid picture of Jeannette as a jealous and rather unstable character. After a number of rows, Brett declared that 'his friendship for Mme Loeser is a thing of the past' (GWD, 10 March 1865, p. 4). In the painting, Jeannette wears a sumptuous dress, with jewellery in the latest fashion. The frame, almost certainly designed by Brett himself, has sleeping cherubs at each corner, presumably intended as emblems of Cupid, the god of love. The painting was finished in August 1864 (implying that Brett saw Jeannette in London in that summer) and was exhibited in Manchester in the autumn of 1865. By this time, however, Alfred Morrison (no. 33) had bought it for £100.
CP

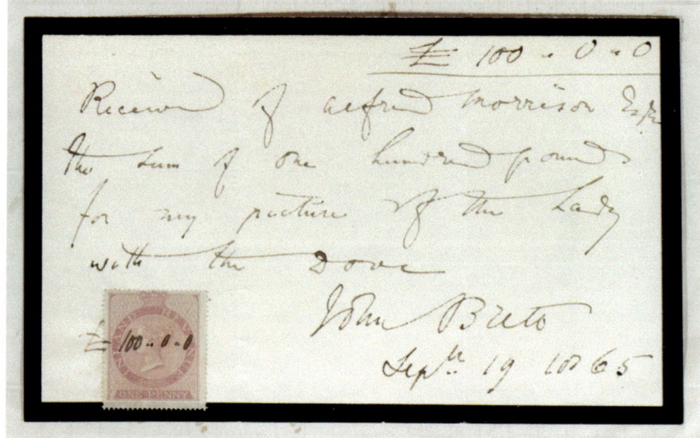
£ 100 . 0 . 0
Received of Alfred Morrison Esq
the sum of one hundred pounds
for my picture of the Lady
with the Dove
£100..0..0
John Brett
Sept 19 1865

Fig. 27 ***Receipt from John Brett***
1865
Lord Margadale of Islay

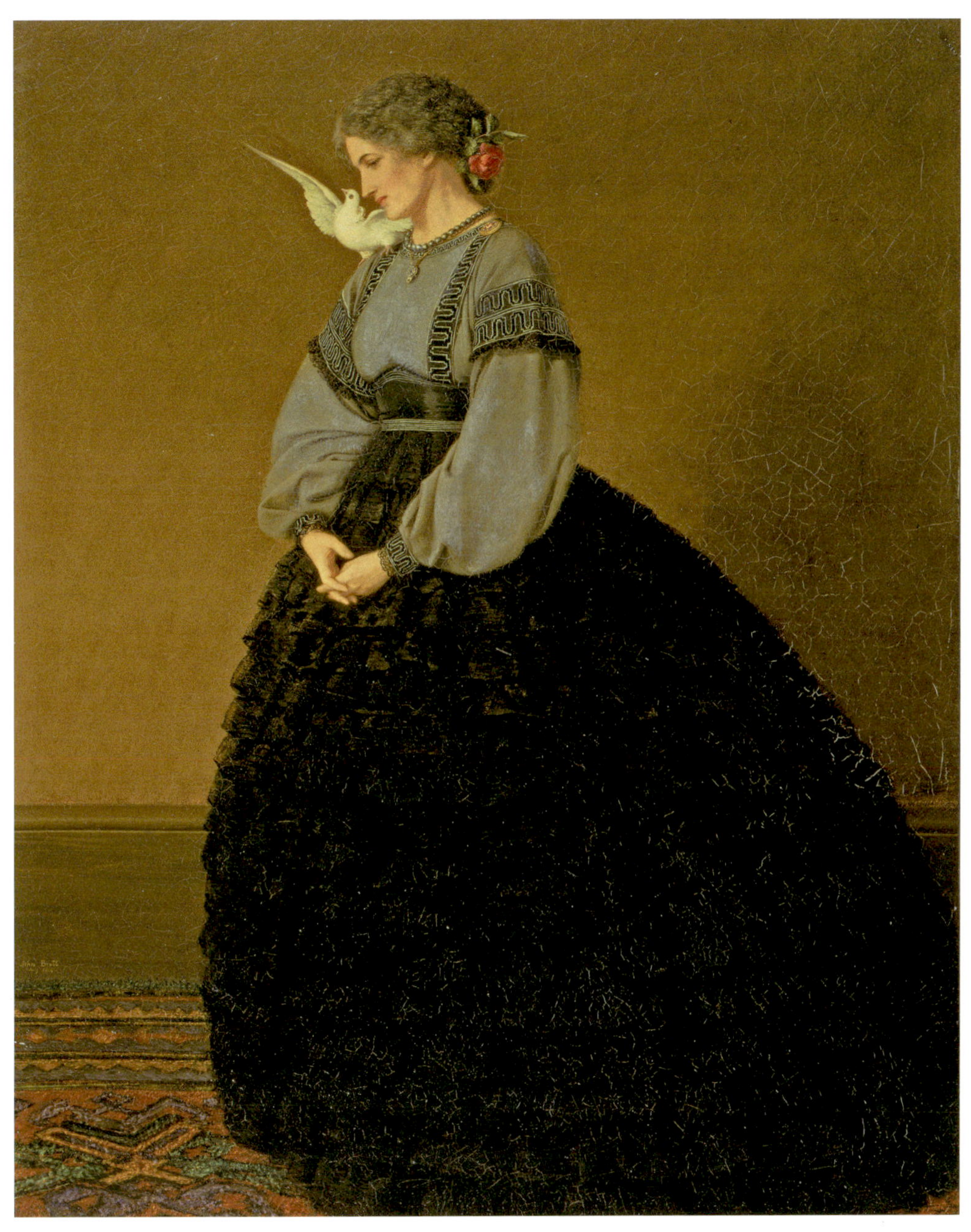

4 ***Ottilie Blind*** **(1869)**

Oil on canvas

61 x 50 cms.

Inscribed: 'J.B. / July1869' l.l.

The Mistress and Fellows of Girton College, Cambridge

In the late 1860s, Brett seems to have been thinking seriously about portraiture in oils: he planned an oil painting of Georgina Weldon in 1866, and had completed one of Mrs Alfred Morrison by 1868. It is likely that he was looking closely at the work of his contemporaries, particularly Whistler and Millais, and in this portrait he adopts a sketchy style which is surprising for an avowed Pre-Raphaelite. Ottilie Blind, later Hancock (1851 - 1929), was the sister of the poet Mathilde Blind, who became close to Ford Madox Brown after 1871, and lived with his family. Ottilie's father was the German revolutionary Karl Blind, and she grew up in a household where regular guests included Marx, Garibaldi and Mazzini. When Brett painted her she was only about 18, but in later life she became a strong supporter of women's suffrage. In 1925 she left £6,000 to Girton College to endow fellowships, one in her own name, and one in that of her great friend Hertha Ayrton, the renowned scientist, who had been the first Jewish woman to study at Cambridge University. There are undated drawings for the portrait in a sketchbook Brett was using between 1868 and 1871 (Sketchbook no. 30, PAF 9435-9); one of these shows Ottilie in profile, standing with her hands crossed below her waist, like Brett's portrait of the *Lady with a Dove* (no. 3). Like Jeannette Loeser, Ottilie had abundant dark hair, and Brett makes the most of it in his portrayal of her. CP

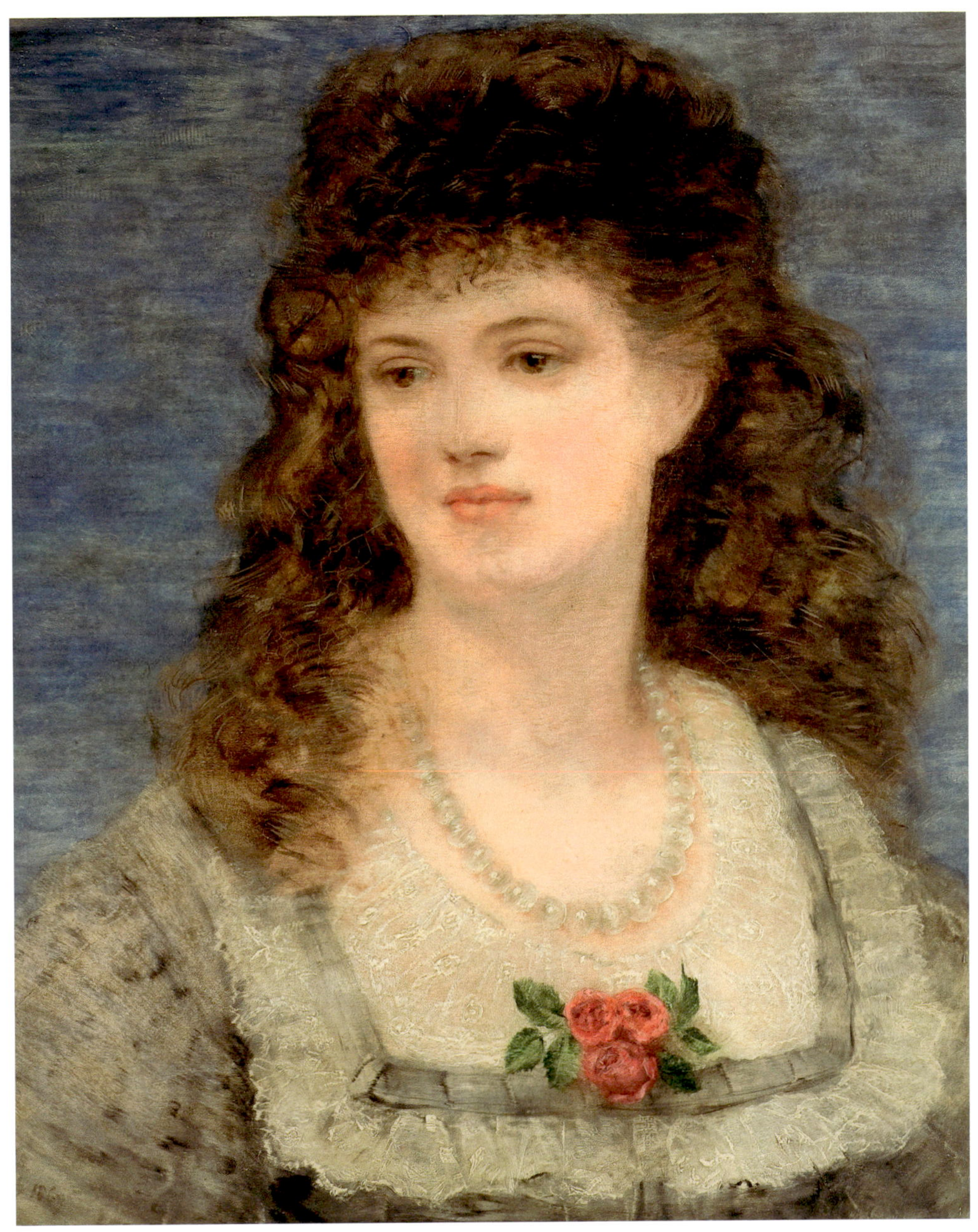

5 ***Mary Brett*** **(1875)**

Oil on canvas

32 x 24.5 cms.

Inscribed: 'JBrett / Sepr 75' l.r.

Private collection

Mary Brett (1843 - 1911) was one of the six children of a coachman. By 1861, when she was 17, she was working away from home as a housemaid (1861 census). After she became attached to John Brett in 1870, however, it seems that she broke off all contact with her family. Her maiden name only became known when one of her descendants found 'Mary Ann Howcroft' inscribed on her Bible (private collection) under a label which had been pasted over it. Brett was following Pre-Raphaelite tradition in choosing a partner from a lower social class. Ford Madox Brown married his model, Emma; Holman Hunt planned to educate Annie Miller so that she could become his wife; Dante Gabriel Rossetti's wife, Lizzie Siddal was a milliner, and William Morris married Jane Burden, the daughter of an 'ostler', whose occupation was probably very similar to that of William Howcroft (Marsh 1985). John and Mary Brett lived together openly as man and wife, but it seems that her background was kept completely secret, even from her own children. It is likely that Brett painted several portraits of her (another one is evident in a photograph of the interior of the Bretts' house in Keswick Road, fig. 28) and he also made many drawings of her in his sketchbooks. However, works such as no. 34 are all quite sketchy, and so far no finished drawings of her have come to light. She was a resourceful character who was obviously devoted to her children, like John Brett himself. CP

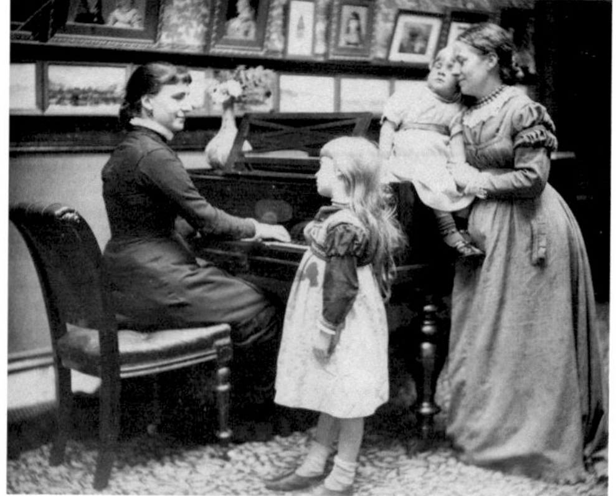

Fig. 28 John Brett, *Mary Brett with Miss Christie, Daisy and Alfred*
About 1878, photograph
Private collection

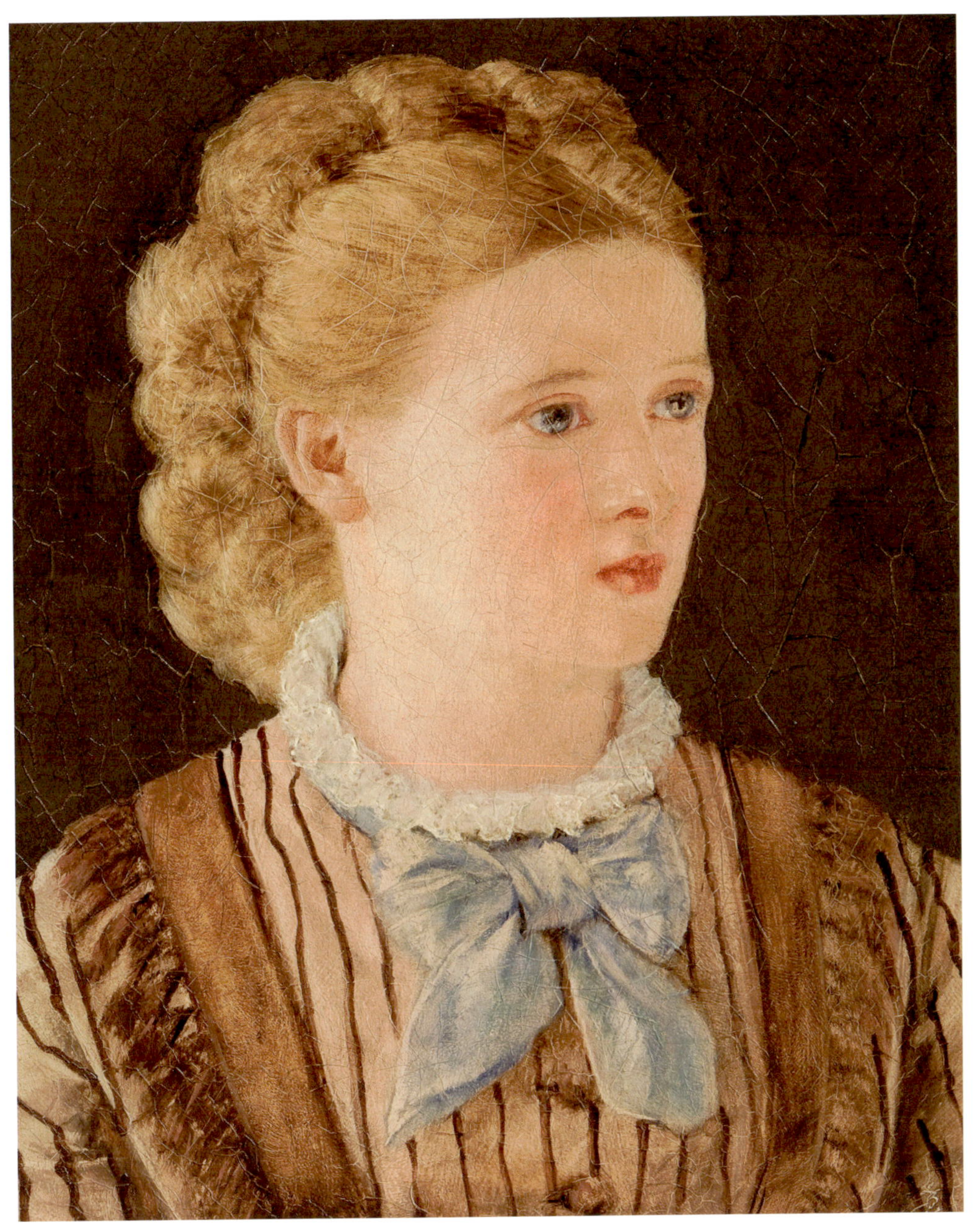

6 *Alfred Brett* (1879)

Oil on canvas
51 x 46 cms.
Inscribed: '1879 John Brett' l.r.
Private collection

This portrait was painted when Alfred Brett (1876 - 1952), known in the family as 'Doll', was two or perhaps just three (he was born in December 1876). His long reddish-blonde hair is still uncut and he wears a dress, as was common practice for young boys in this period before they were 'breeched', that is put into trousers at the age of three or four. In this year the family spent the summer in Penally, near Tenby, and Brett wrote of Alfred: 'Doll is supremely beautiful and as good as beautiful. He is now allowed up to taste dinner with the others and having tasted he goes off in the dark to bed without a hint, like a little lamb, leaving the others to carouse in the candlelight' (ET, 5 October 1879, p. 5). A photograph Brett took of Alfred, a few years later (fig. 29), shows a marked change in his demeanour from the unruly toddler he had photographed about 1878 (fig. 12). As he grew up Alfred showed an aptitude for science: in 1889, when he was 12, Brett bought him an Altazimuth in the hope that he might one day become Astronomer Royal (ibid., 14 April 1889, p. 54). Like his brothers Michael and Spencer, Alfred went to Winchester College. When he left, in 1894, Brett could not afford to send him to Oxford, but enrolled him in the Royal College of Science instead (ibid., 9 June 1896, p. 74). In later life he became a mining engineer, working in Celebes (Dutch East India) and then in South Africa. CP

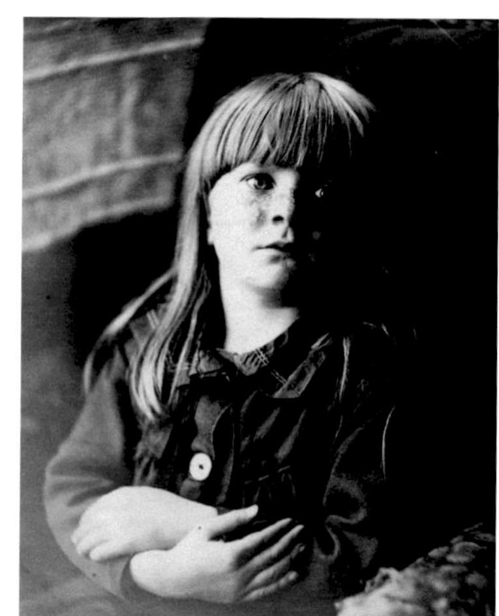

Fig. 29 John Brett, *Alfred Brett*
About 1882, photograph
Private collection

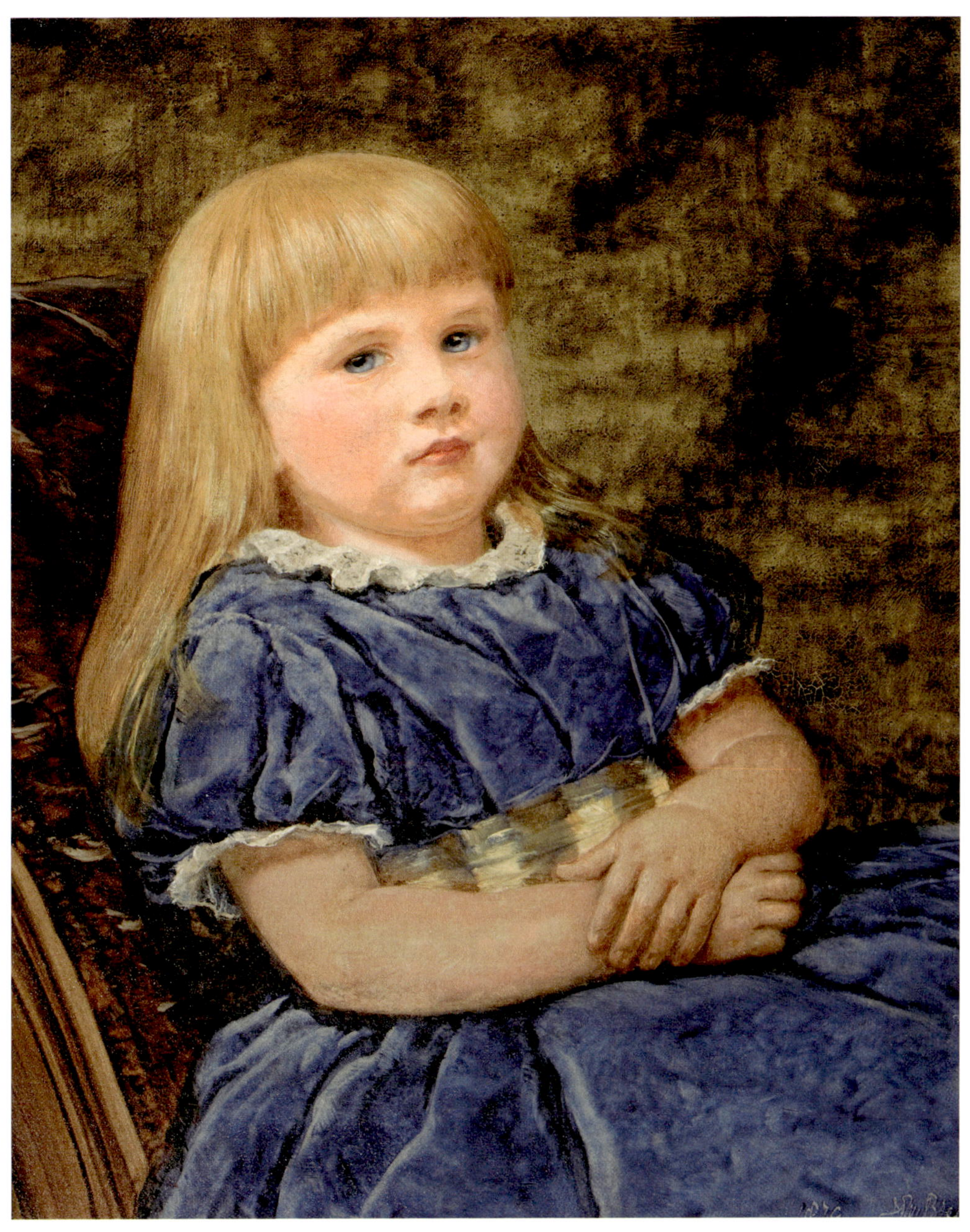

7 *Pansy Brett* (1882)

Oil on canvas

37.3 x 33 cms.

Inscribed: 'Pansy Brett / July 28 1882' l.l.

Private collection

Brett painted many portraits of his children. They can be seen hanging above the dado rail, alongside his oil sketches, in photographs of the central hall of the family house in Keswick Road (fig. 28). This portrait of Pansy (1878 - 1932) was painted soon after her fourth birthday in July 1882. In this summer the family was staying in Newport Castle, on the coast of Pembrokeshire. The day before he finished the portrait, Brett wrote in the family journal: 'We now have seven children and they are all in superb health ... They are as good and beautiful as they are healthy. They radiate pleasure on all they meet and fill the lives of their parents with delightful days and their outlook with delightful dreams' (ET, 27 July 1882, p. 11). A year later he wrote of Pansy, then aged five, that she acted as a 'little mother' to the others, 'telling when they are in danger, finding their things when they are lost and charming everyone with her sweet, sensible little remarks, and the merry chirp of her sweet unconscious voice' (ET, 2 September 1883, p. 20). Pansy's dress and pose have obvious affinities with the famous *Cherry Ripe* by Millais (1879, private collection), a painter whom Brett greatly admired. 1882 may be seen as the peak of Brett's career, when his paintings were selling easily and for very high prices, and he was able to afford to send his sons to expensive boarding schools. The girls were educated at home by a succession of governesses, and then attended a day school in Putney. CP

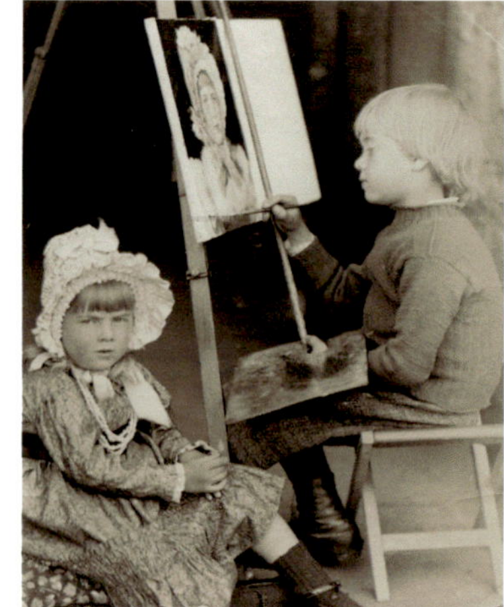

Fig. 30 John Brett, *Pansy Posing for Jasper*
1882, photograph
Private collection

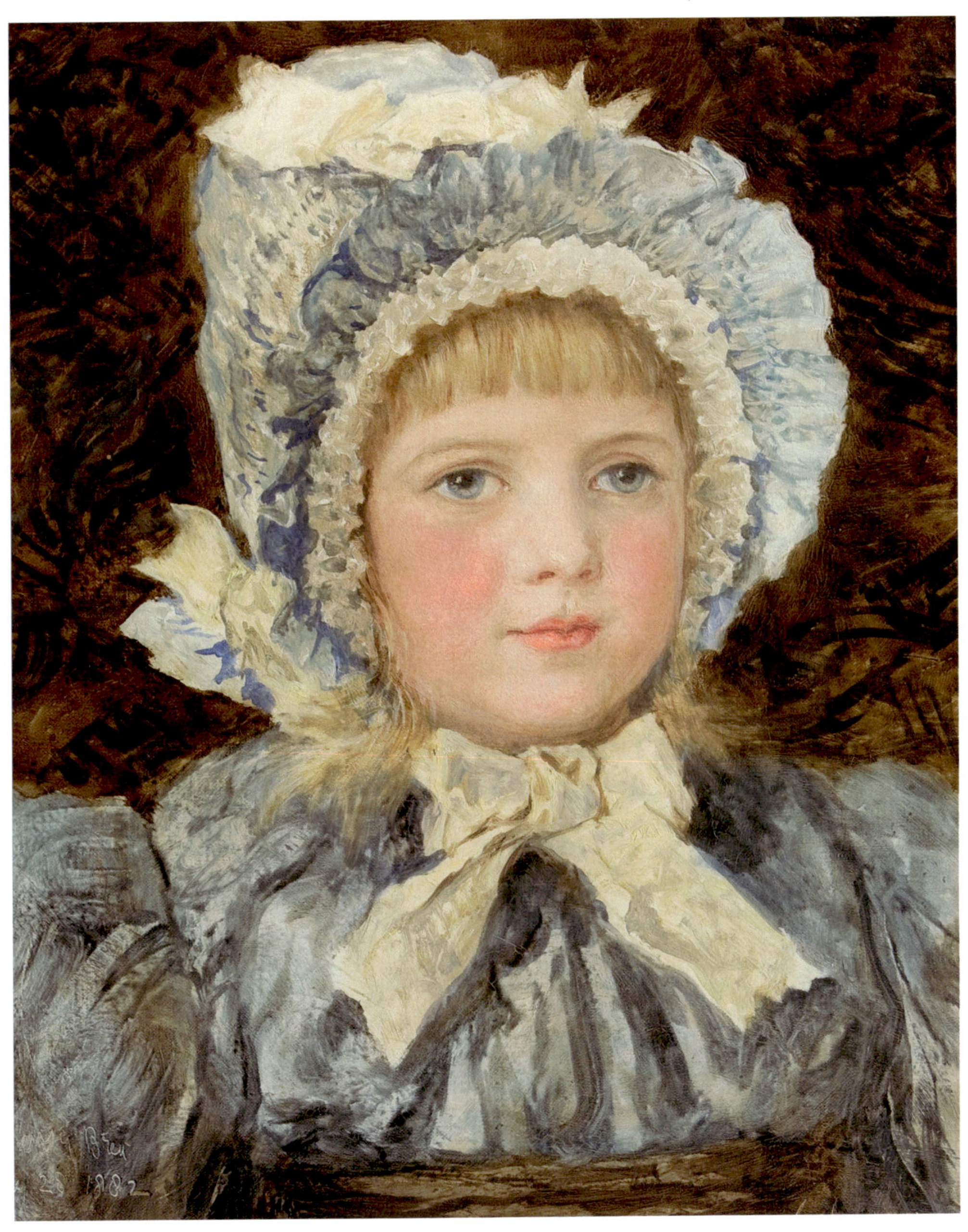

8 ***Gwendolen Brett* (1888)**

Oil on panel
35 x 30 cms.
Inscribed: 'Gwendolen Brett aged 6' l.l. and 'John Brett 1888' l.r.
Private collection

This portrait of the Bretts' youngest child Gwendolen (1882 - 1915), painted when she was six, is, like the portrait of Pansy, a tribute to Millais's *Cherry Ripe*. In his Studio Log, Brett notes that he began the portrait on 31 August 1888 'on a panel that had been in the house 8 years' (SL). At this time, Brett was thoroughly depressed by his growing inability to sell his landscapes, but he was greatly cheered up by the exploits of his children. A few days before he began this portrait he wrote: 'Gwendolen still leads the whole crew. Her talk is the chief charm of the breakfast table. She is very inventive and has a little Familiar whom she refers to as her double, and who has power of magic. She is called "Sim". She also has divers other little attendant spirits. Gwen is ready at a name for everything, even her mother she calls "Scobie", I don't know the origin of this' (ET, 26 August 1888, p. 51). In 1896 Brett recorded with great pride Gwen's success in the Cambridge preliminary examination, when she was one of only four girls in the entire country to take honours in the First Class (ibid., 9 June 1896, p. 75). CP

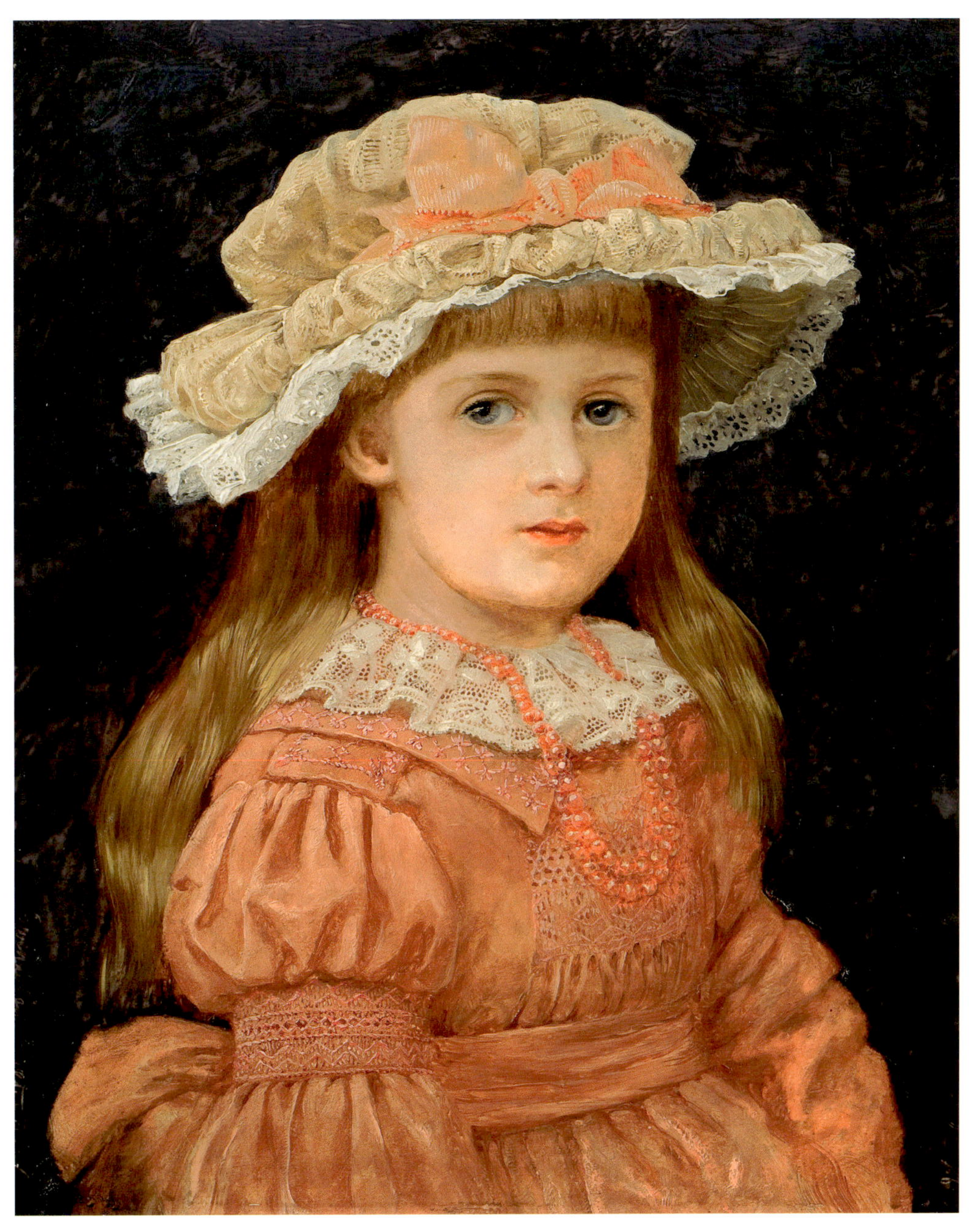

Works on Paper

9 ***Portrait of a Woman (Eliza Orme?)*** **(about 1854/5)**
Charcoal and stump on paper
35.4 x 25.6 cms.
The Trustees of The British Museum, London

This portrait was formerly in one of the Brett family collections. It has no inscription, and the identification of the sitter as Mrs Orme is not certain, but seems very likely. Eliza Orme was the wife of Charles Orme, a prosperous distiller, the sister of Emily Patmore, and the sister-in-law of John Brett's aunt, Caroline Brett. In his early diary John mentions frequent visits to her house, starting in July 1851. Eliza Orme had a salon at which she entertained writers, thinkers and artists, including the young Pre-Raphaelites. William Michael Rossetti described her as 'a lady ... of rich physique, with luminous dark eyes [who] had a refined taste and a great liking for the society of writers and artists' (Rossetti 1906, vol. i, p. 89). The composition of this drawing is similar to Millais's oil portrait of Emily Patmore (fig. 3), with the lace collar and ribbon at her throat, the focus on the eyes and the apparent exaggeration of her long nose and narrow face. The media, a combination of charcoal and stump, are unusual for Brett, but there is a drawing of Edwin in the same materials which must be of similar date (private collection). Brett recorded his opinion of Mrs Orme in his diary: 'She is a highly intellectual woman & cultivated & facinating withal' (JBD, 15 September 1853, p. 47). CP

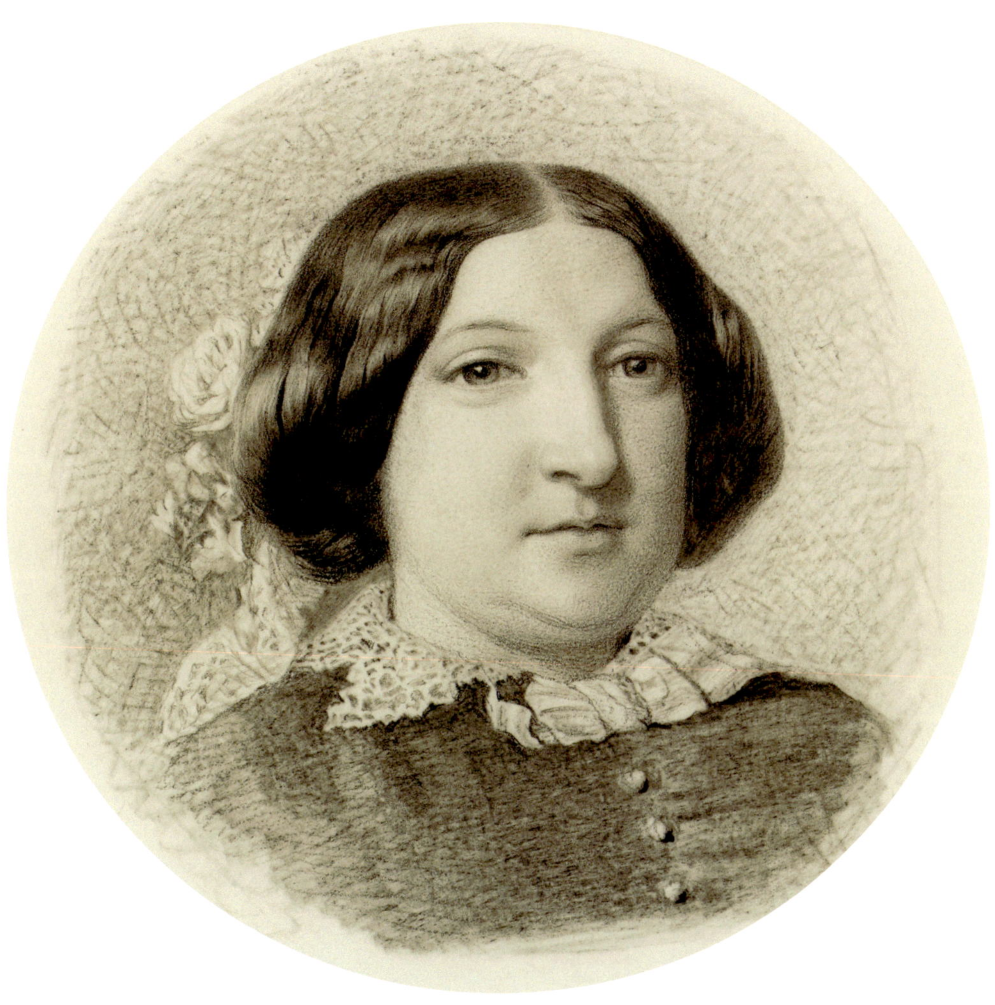

10 *Arthur Brett* (1855-6)

Pencil on paper
19 x 16.5 cms.
Inscribed: 'John Brett / Dec^{r} &c 1855-6' l.l.
Exhibited: Royal Academy, London, 1856, no. 988
Private collection

This portrait of Brett's brother Arthur is one of at least four finely finished portrait drawings he made in 1855, and it was one of his first three exhibits at the annual Royal Academy exhibition in 1856. Such detailed pencil portraits were popular in late 18th- and early to mid-19th-century Britain, and it is likely that Brett exhibited this drawing in the hope that it would lead to commissions. However, there was plenty of competition, not least from the relatively new form of portraiture provided by the daguerreotype. The drawing may be compared with William Holman Hunt's portrait of Millais in pastel and chalk (1853, National Portrait Gallery, London). The composition is very similar, although there is more shadow on the face in Brett's drawing. Also, while Millais's eyes gaze straight ahead, Arthur's are downcast. This is a feature of a number of Brett's portrait drawings, suggesting that the sitter is lost in thought or concentrating on a task. CP

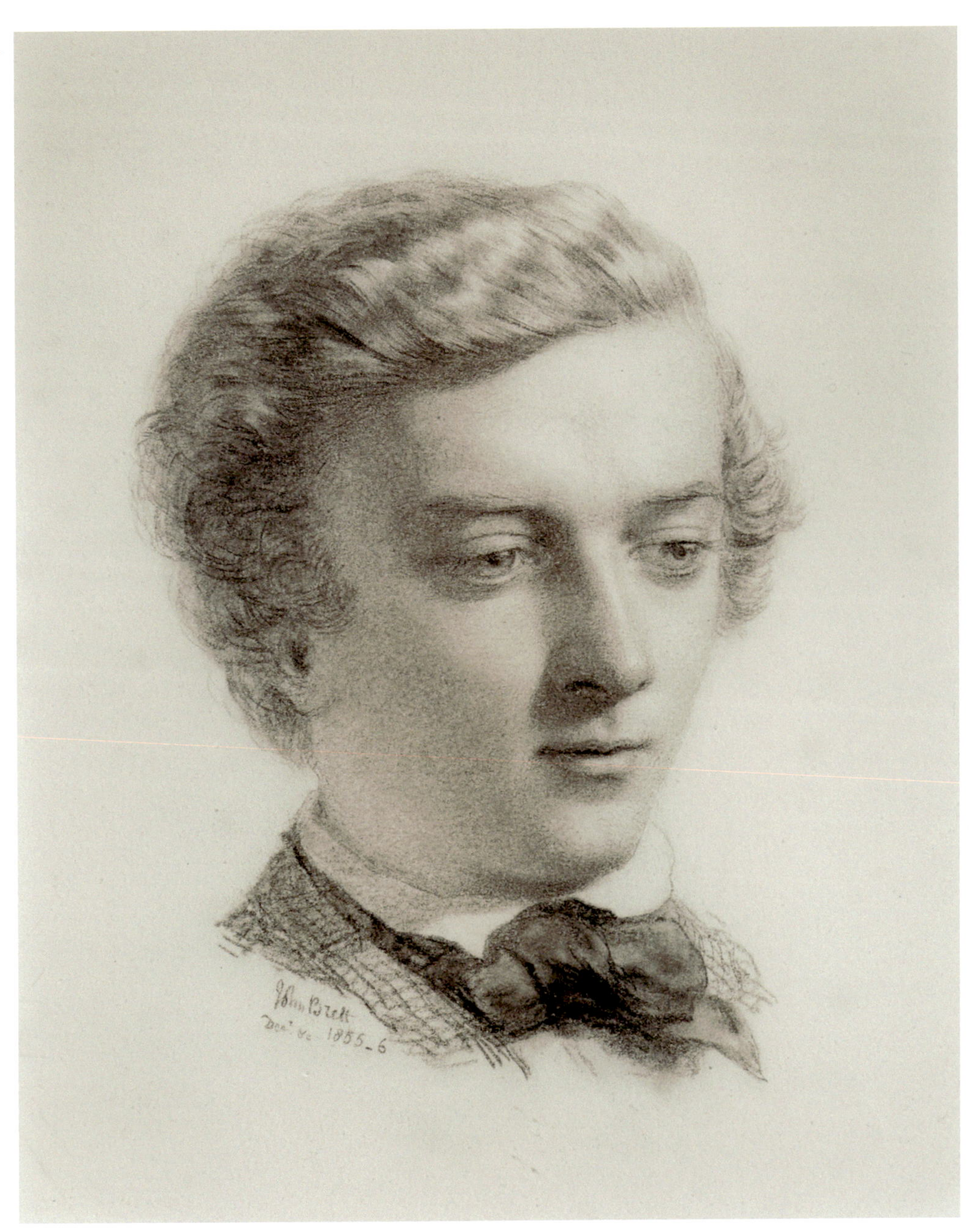
John Brett
1855-6

11 *Theodore Brett* (1858)

Etching

10 x 8.9 cms.

Inscribed: 'JB Feb 3 / 58' l.l.

Private collection

This etching of Brett's brother Theodore (1833 - 1883) is based on a pen drawing of 1855 (private collection). It could have been reproduced in multiple copies to circulate amongst family members, although no other impressions are known at present. Brett's finely hatched pen and ink style was well suited to translation into etching, and there are several references in his diaries to his use of the technique. Theodore is a mysterious figure. He seems to have had no profession, although there are indications that he was to learn farming. He may have had a learning disability, or he may simply have been dyslexic. In a letter to his sister Rosa, written in 1854 (private collection), John discusses suitable professions for Theodore, including being a clerk to an architect: 'I don't know if Tib [his nickname] cd draw plans better than he cd write'. By 1860, however, he was at home and growing stouter, 'having nothing to do' (JBD, 1 January 1860, p. 66). In later life he lived with his sister Rosa. He survived her by only one year. CP

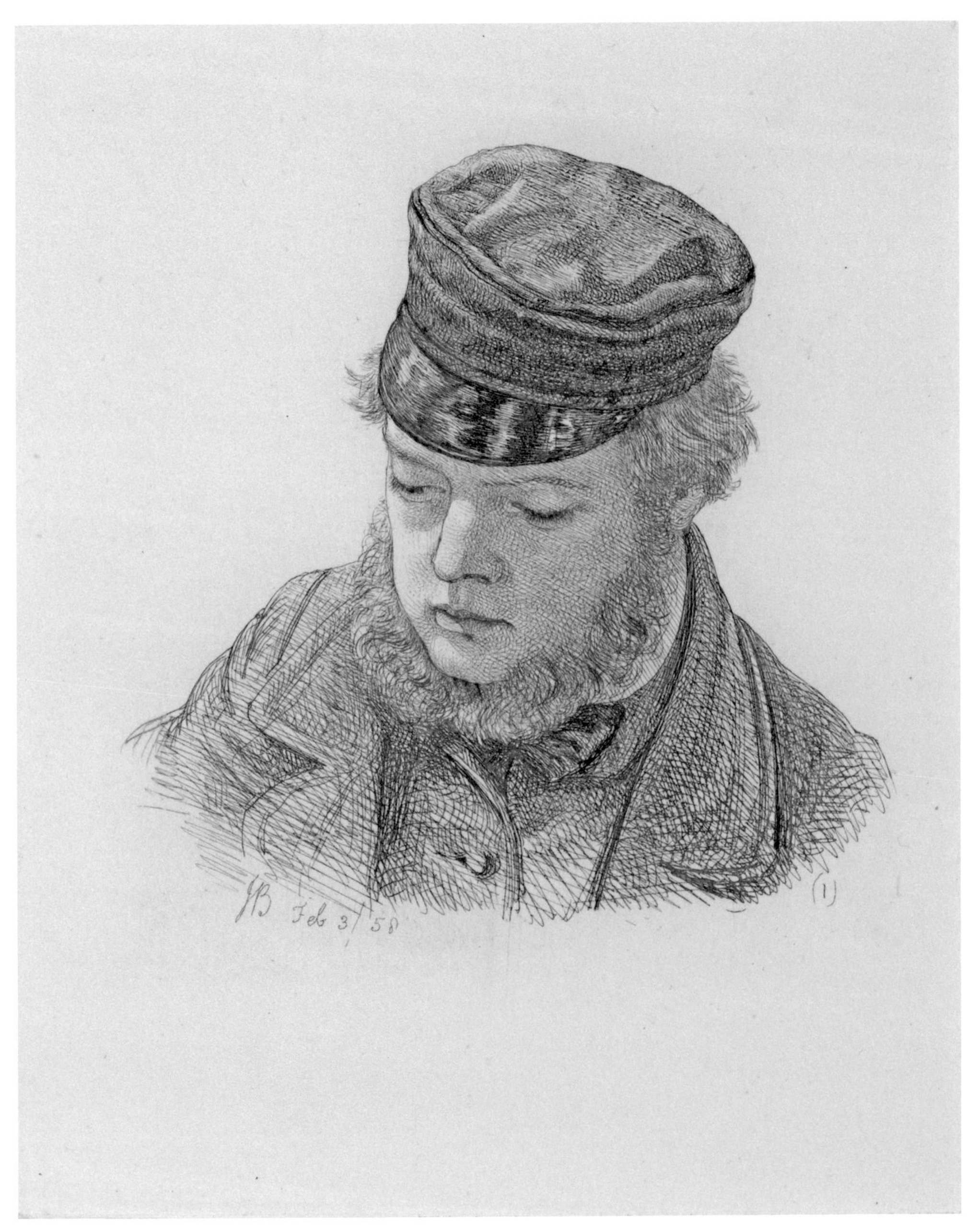
JB Feb 3/58
(1)

12 **_Self Portrait_ (1858)**

Pen and ink and bodycolour on light brown paper
20.5 x 13.5 cms.
Inscribed: 'Château de st Pierre / Novr. 1. 1858' l.r.
Private collection

Brett stayed at the Château de St Pierre while he was working on his most ambitious painting, the *Val d'Aosta* (fig. 2). He executed this self portrait towards the end of his stay there, perhaps to mark his completion of the painting (he had drawn a similar self portrait a year before, at about the time he completed the *Stonebreaker* (fig. 1)). The intensity of his gaze is comparable to self portraits by artists of the Romantic generation, such as the famous example by Samuel Palmer (The Ashmolean Museum, Oxford). Brett's self portraits, however, emphasise his clear-sightedness and have an air of pride and certainty, perhaps conveying those aspects of his character which had led Ruskin to write 'my sitting room is big enough for both - providing you don't argue above eight hours a day' when he invited Brett to stay with him in Turin earlier in that summer (letter dated 14 August 1858, private collection). Brett has used pen and ink, sketching in the shaggy hair and beard quite roughly, but deploying extremely fine strokes for the eyes. The highlights, in white bodycolour, now more prominent because the paper has darkened, add to the liveliness of the image. CP

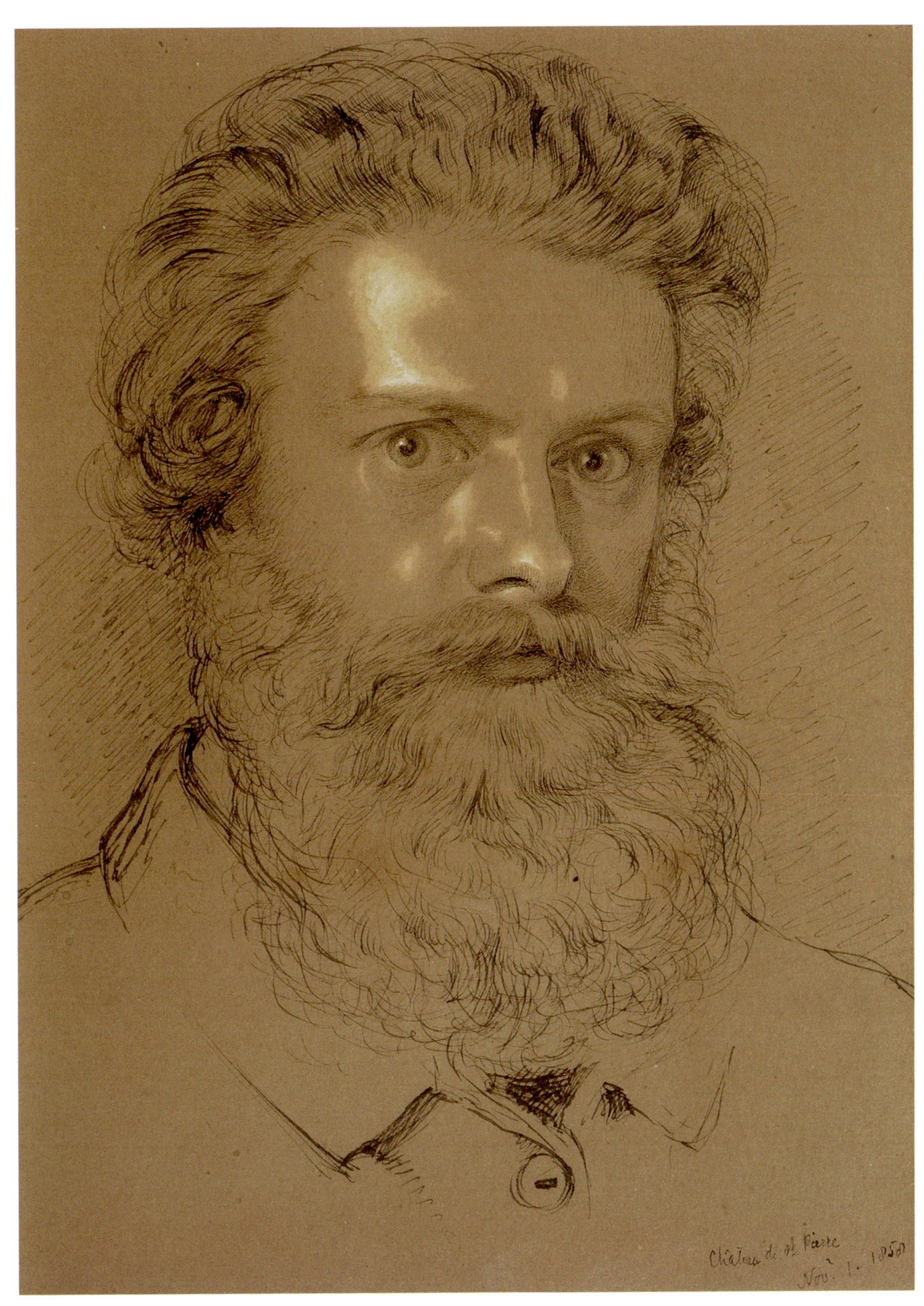

13 *Arthur Hughes* (1858)

Pencil on paper
20.6 x 22.2 cms.
Inscribed: 'Arthur Hughes' t.r. and 'Decr 9 58' l.r.
The National Portrait Gallery, London

Arthur Hughes (1832 - 1915) moved to Maidstone in the summer of 1858, with his Maidstone-born wife and two children. Brett returned from the Valle d'Aosta in November of that year, and stayed at the family house in Detling, near Maidstone for much of the following year. During this time he probably saw a lot of Hughes: they were working on similar subjects, focusing on the life of agricultural labourers. The similarity in the main figures for Brett's *Hedger* (fig. 8) and Hughes's *Home from Work* (Forbes Magazine Collection) strongly suggests that the two artists worked side by side, sharing the same model (Roberts and Wildman 1997, pp. 13, 16). This is a finely executed drawing which conveys Hughes's reserved and sensitive nature. Presumably, Brett drew him when he was at work, hence the downcast eyes and air of concentration. It is not known whether Brett and Hughes kept in touch in the intervening years, but much later on, in 1889, they were together in Cornwall, where, once again, they probably sketched side by side (Fredeman 1967, p. 22). CP

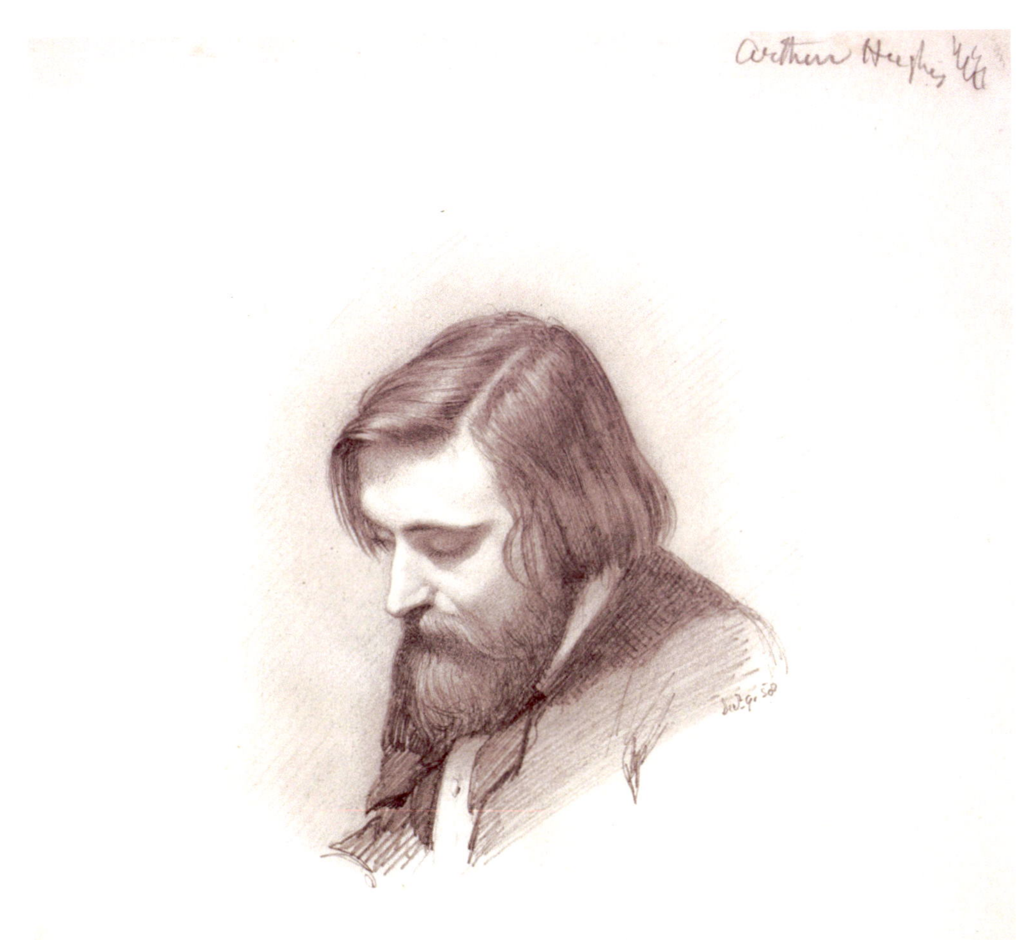

14 *Edwin Brett* (1858)

Red chalk and bodycolour on paper
17.8 x 15.2 cms.
Inscribed: 'Portrait of / Edwin Brett' l.l. and 'JB / Decr 24. 1858' l.r.
Private collection

This drawing of John Brett's youngest brother, Edwin (1841 - 1919), was made on Christmas Eve, when the family was at Detling for what Brett feared was to be their last Christmas together. Just over a year earlier, Edwin had modelled for the figure of a boy breaking stones in Brett's first critical success, the *Stonebreaker* (fig. 1). In December 1858, John wrote in his diary 'Edwin is yet much of a child and that keeps us children', but Edwin had already joined the army, as a Cornet (junior officer) in the 3rd Dragoon Guards, in the summer of 1858 (JBD, 25 December 1858, p. 64). A year later he was indeed missing from the family group, being on his way out to India. Brett used red chalk for this drawing, a material well suited to conveying the warmth and softness of flesh. Unusually for Brett, Edwin stares straight out at the viewer, his steady gaze and firm mouth suggesting the resolve of a young man who has recently decided on an army career. In adulthood, Edwin shared John Brett's passion for yachting; the two brothers travelled together on Brett's first yacht, the *Baby*, in 1866 (no. 37), and in 1869, Edwin published a book, *Notes on Yachts*, which had a frontispiece by John. CP

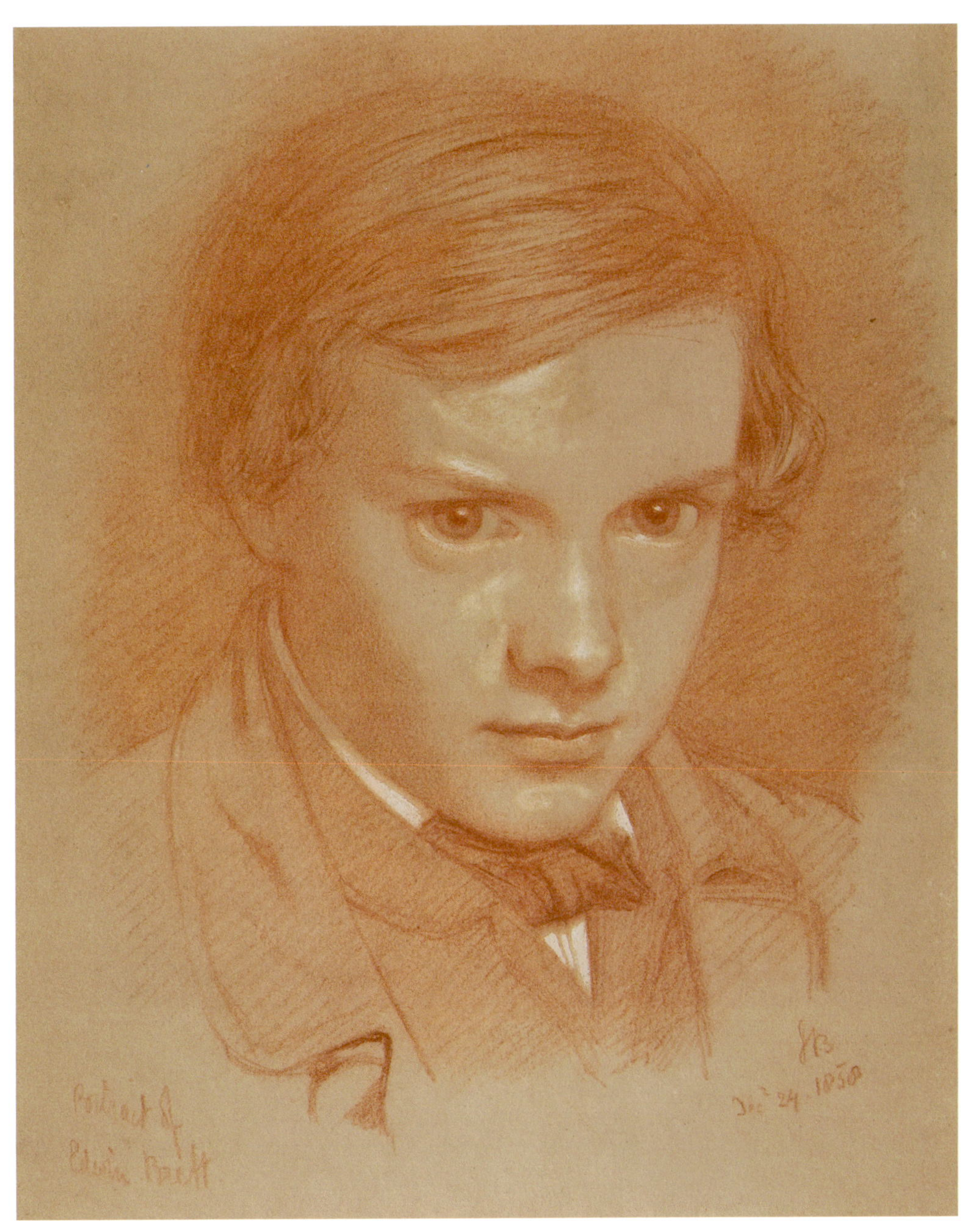

15 *Emma Brett* (1859)

Red chalk on paper
44 x 34 cms.
Inscribed: 'Emma' u.c., 'Jan 3 1859 JB' l.l.
Private collection

As far as we know, this is the largest drawing John Brett ever made in red chalk, a medium that was particularly favoured by artists for its subtlety and often used by Dante Gabriel Rossetti. Emma Brett (1832 - 1902) was John's cousin, the eldest child of his father's brother, George Brett. He has chosen to portray her holding a piece of material as if sewing, a pose that would have been easy to maintain, but also one which conformed to the ideal of female gentleness and industriousness. This drawing was made in January 1859, when Emma had perhaps been staying with the Bretts over New Year. The following year, 1860, she was there to take the place of Ann Brett, who was ill. John Brett confided to his diary that she 'does everything very silently and kindly but her face is deeply melancholy. I seldom speak to her, greatly as I respect her. I cant help heartily wishing she were away' (JBD, 25 December 1858, p. 64). It is not clear whether he wished Emma away because of her melancholy face, or because her presence meant the illness of his mother. It may be significant that in this drawing he chose to show very little of her face, and it is difficult to read any expression beyond one of quiet concentration. CP

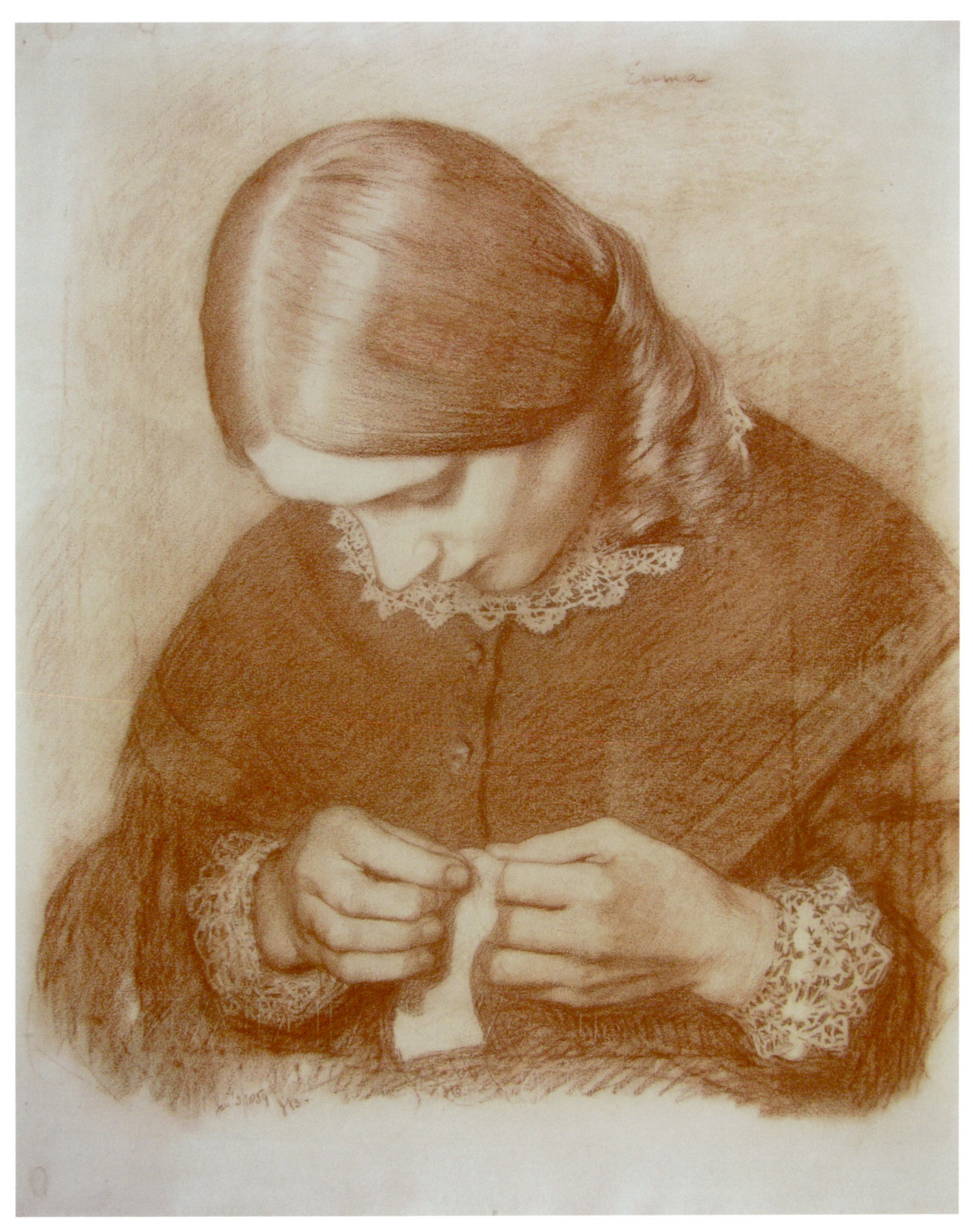

16 ***Study for The Hedger* (1858/9)**

Monochrome wash and bodycolour on paper
25 x 18.5 cms.
Private collection

This detailed, undated study for an oil painting is unique in Brett's work. It has been argued (Gridley and Hickox 2001) that Brett made the drawing in spring 1858, in order to seek an opinion on it at a meeting with Ruskin in April of that year, but there is no definite evidence that it took place. If Brett had consulted Ruskin, he would probably have been advised not to proceed, since the critic thought the subject 'wholly uninteresting' (letter to Thomas Plint, John Rylands Library, University of Manchester, about 1860, 1254 letter 15). It may have been executed in the early spring of 1859, after Brett had made a rapid sketch of the composition of *The Hedger* on 18 May 1858 (private collection, Staley and Newall 2004, p. 186), and before he started work on the oil version, which was exhibited at the Royal Academy in 1860 and at the RBSA in 1865 (fig. 8). However, the monochrome is much closer in design and content to this 18 May 1858 sketch, than to the final oil painting. Brett used two models, both of them local labourers. The first and older model was Stephen Waghorn (born about 1781). In his diary entry for 31 July 1859 Brett noted that 'the poor old fellow who sat for the outline and was to have served as model throughout died yesterday' (JBD, p. 65). The second and younger model was William Swift (born about 1823), whose twelve year-old daughter, Alice, was living with the Bretts as their servant in 1861. CP

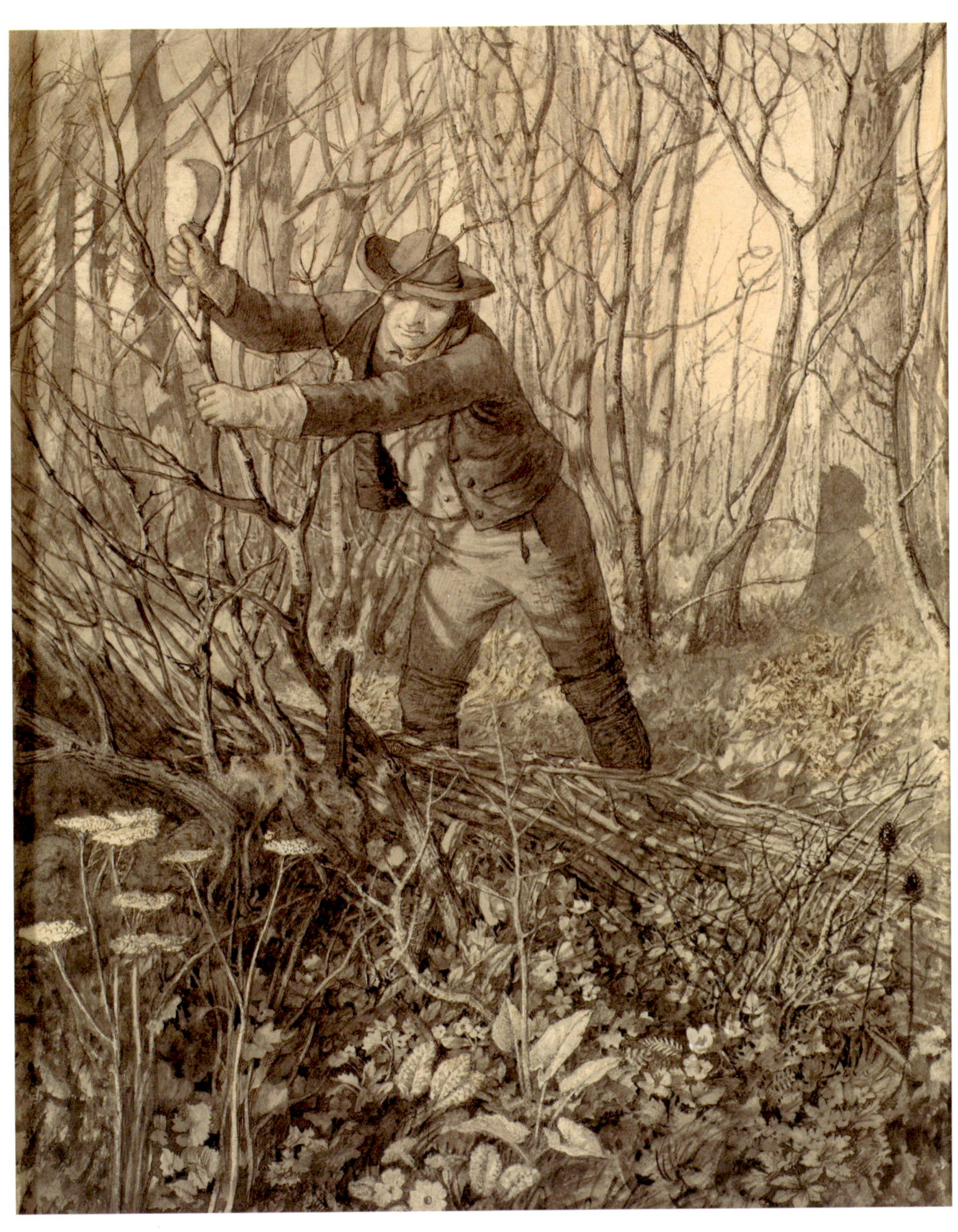

17 ***Ann Brett* (1859)**

Pen and ink on paper
22.9 x 19.7 cms.
Inscribed: 'Decr 27.59' l.r.
Private collection

John Brett's mother, née Ann Pilbeam (1807 - 1874), appears to have been a self-effacing character about whom little is known. He describes her in his early diary only as 'my dear good sensible Mother', while he is considerably more enthusiastic about his father, 'my chief pride & glory' (JBD, 16 August 1853, p. 43). This pen and ink drawing of her gives a vivid impression of the restricted domestic roles reserved for women in the 19th century: they were expected to be calm, dignified and submissive, an 'angel in the house' providing a peaceful and secure base from which their husbands and children could venture into the world outside. She is depicted reading by the fireside, in a well-appointed, middle-class interior, as the linchpin of a domestic circle. Brett had been devoting much effort to pen and ink drawings in 1859, perhaps hoping to get work as an illustrator: the medium can be translated very effectively by the technique of wood engraving. The drawing was made when members of the family were at home together for Christmas. Five days later, on New Year's Day 1860, Brett wrote that his mother was ill and cousin Emma had come to take her place at the head of domestic affairs (ibid., 1 January 1860, p. 66). CP

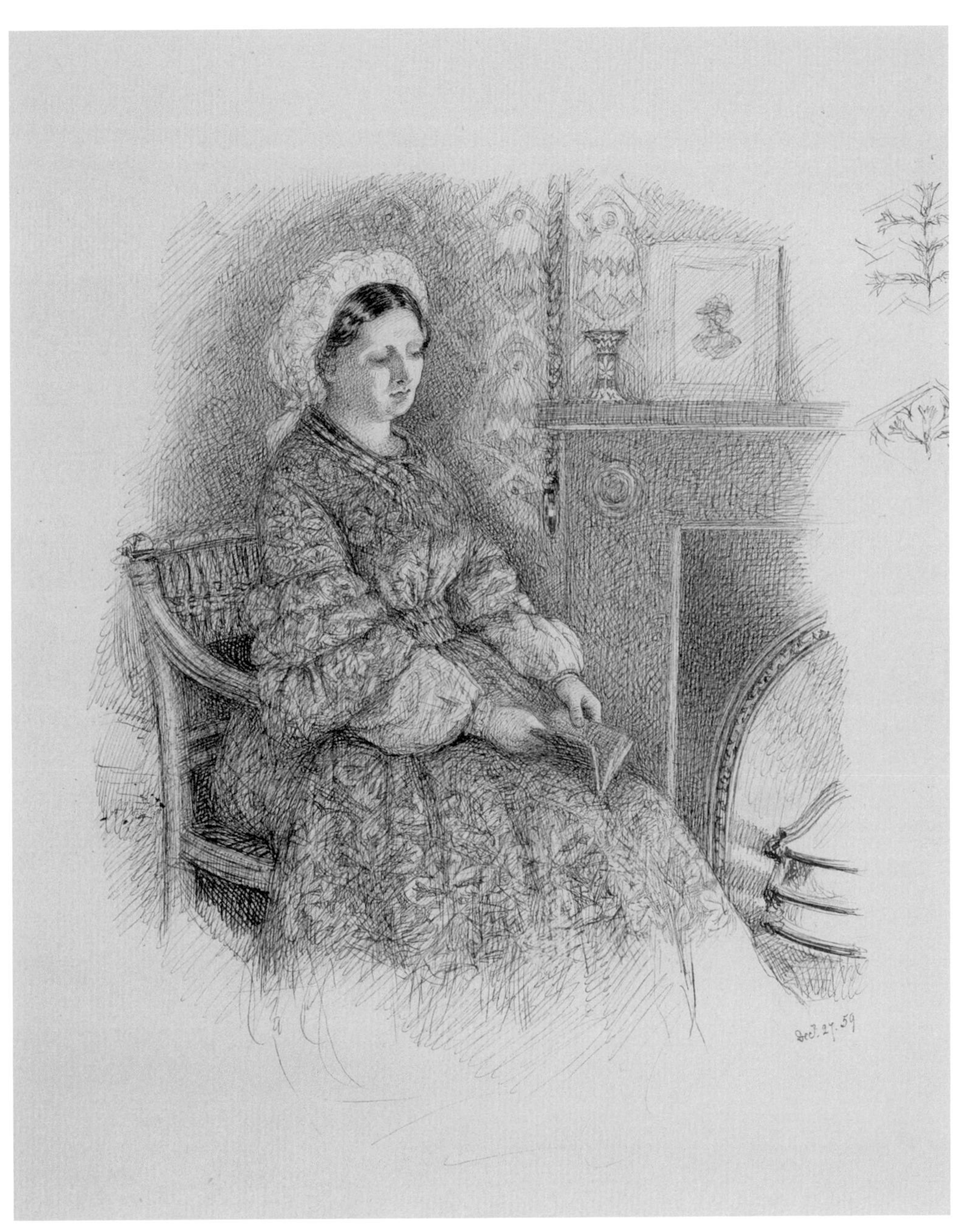
Dec. 27. 59

18 *Georgina Hannay* (1859)

Pen and ink on paper
22.8 x 20.3 cms.
Inscribed: 'J.B. / Decr. 29. 59' l.r.
The Ashmolean Museum, Oxford

Like the drawing of his mother (no. 17) this pen and ink study of Georgina Hannay, Brett's future sister-in-law, suggests the confined domestic world of the mid-19th-century woman. The potted plants, perhaps geraniums, and her pose and expression, help convey a languid, hothouse atmosphere. Georgina was to marry Arthur Brett in 1862, but in January 1860, a few days after he made this drawing, John's diary entry implies that he was in love with her too: 'her sweet voice and brilliant wit and lovely temper do a wonderful deal towards keeping away the gloom that would hang over us [his mother was ill and Edwin on his way to India, his most recent letter received two months earlier], and also do a great deal towards making me feel dreary and spooney. When shall I leave off being a fool! There is no improvement I am just as weak and ungovernable as ever, and like an infant, experience stiff enough one would have thought to tame a bear is simply thrown away on me' (JBD, 1 January 1860, p. 66). CP

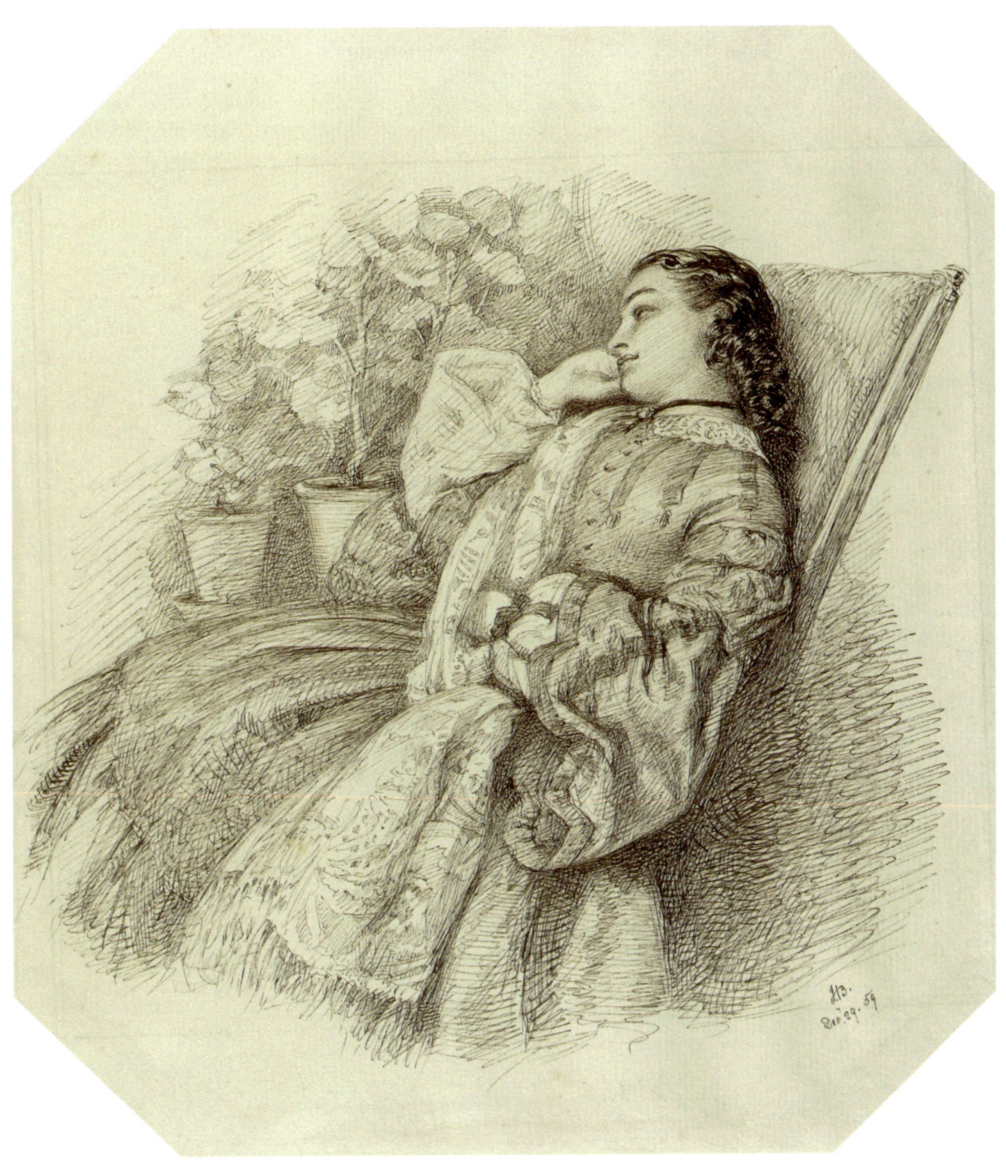
Dec. 29. 59

19 ***Charles Curtis Brett* (1859)**

Pen and ink on paper

24.1 x 22.2 cms.

Inscribed: 'John Brett / Decr 30 1859' l.r.

Private collection

John Brett had a deep affection and great respect for his father, Charles Curtis Brett (1789 - 1865). John describes this drawing in his diary on New Year's Day 1860: 'I made a pen drawing of his head a few days ago, never more beautiful and fresh, and with elastic curl in his lovely grey locks' (JBD, 1 January 1860, p. 66). In his Studio Log, begun in 1887, John specifically mentions this drawing - '4 portraits and the pen and ink portrait of my father' - presumably hanging on the wall (SL, B2). It seems likely, therefore, that he kept it in a prominent position - watching over him, as it were, perhaps until the end of his life. When his children were growing up, Charles Curtis Brett was a veterinary surgeon in the army, but he had served in the navy as a young man, and was also an accomplished painter and musician. He was an important role model for his son in many ways, not least in the interest he took in his sons and daughter. Other drawings and photographs of Charles Curtis show that he had a facial paralysis on his left side, possibly as a result of Parkinson's Disease (fig. 5). The profile view chosen by Brett for this vigorous drawing conceals this handicap and shows him in the prime of life. CP

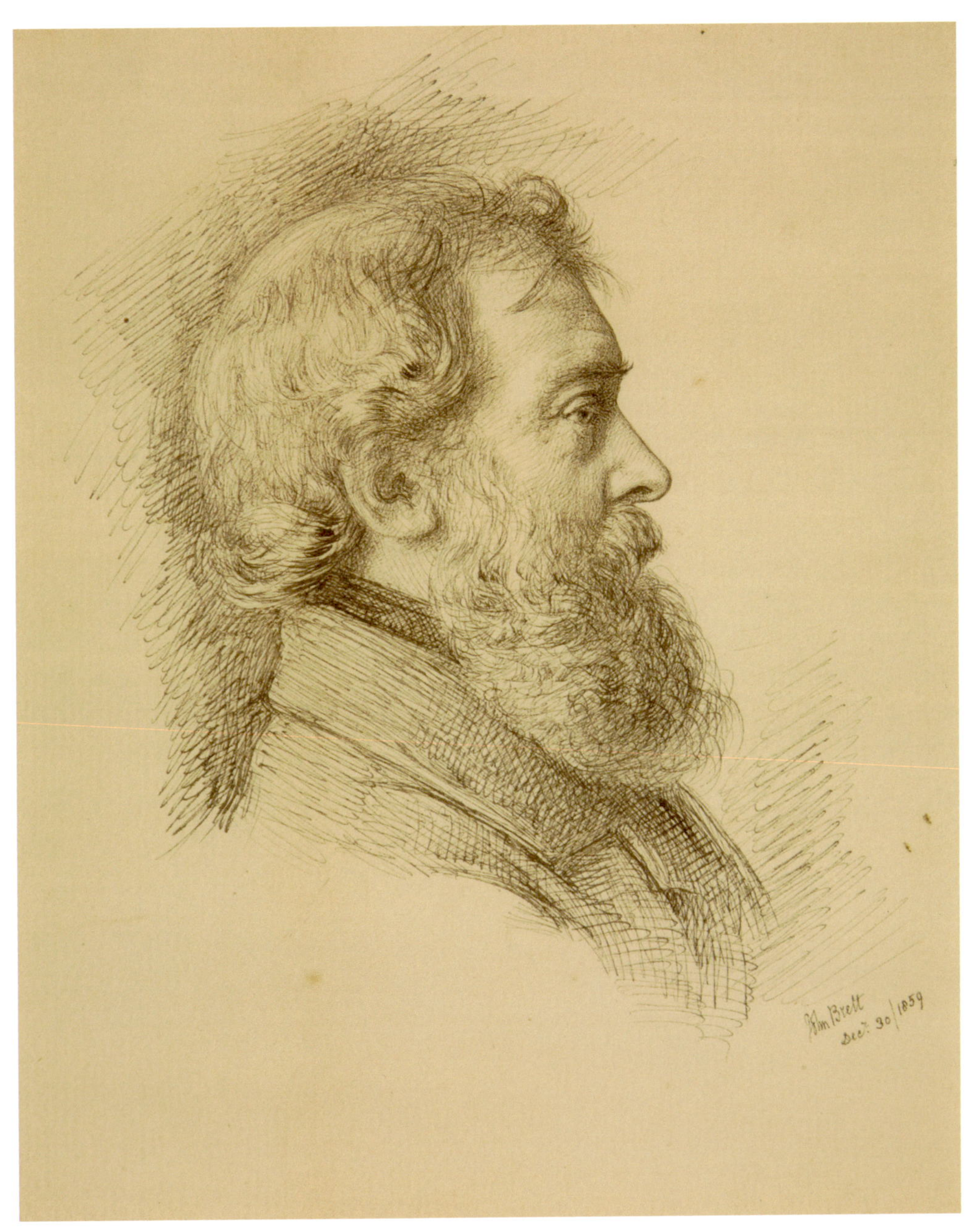
Wm Brett
Decr. 30/1859

20 ***Laura Epps, later Alma-Tadema* (1860)**

Watercolour and bodycolour on paper
17.8 x 15.8 cms.
Inscribed: 'J B 1860' l.l. and 'J B / 1860' l.r.
The Ashmolean Museum, Oxford

Laura Epps (1852 - 1909) was the daughter of Dr George Epps, the homeopath. It is likely that the Brett and Epps families were friends. Brett was a keen homeopath himself, and he gave drawing lessons to Laura and her sisters (Marsh 1994, p. 204). In February 1861, Laura's older sister Emily was modelling for him (JBD, p. 68). Laura became a successful artist in later life, and when she married the painter Lawrence Alma-Tadema in 1871, John Brett was one of the witnesses, the others being her parents and brother (Dixon 2006, p. 73). This delicate watercolour portrait of Laura is unique in Brett's work. Whether it was a commission or a gift, he evidently took great pains over it, deftly using a combination of watercolour and bodycolour to bring out the varied colours in her coppery hair and the reflected lights on her grey jacket, setting them off against the complementary blue of the cushion. He took particular trouble in delineating the pale lashes against her gleaming eyes, which seem lost in reverie. CP

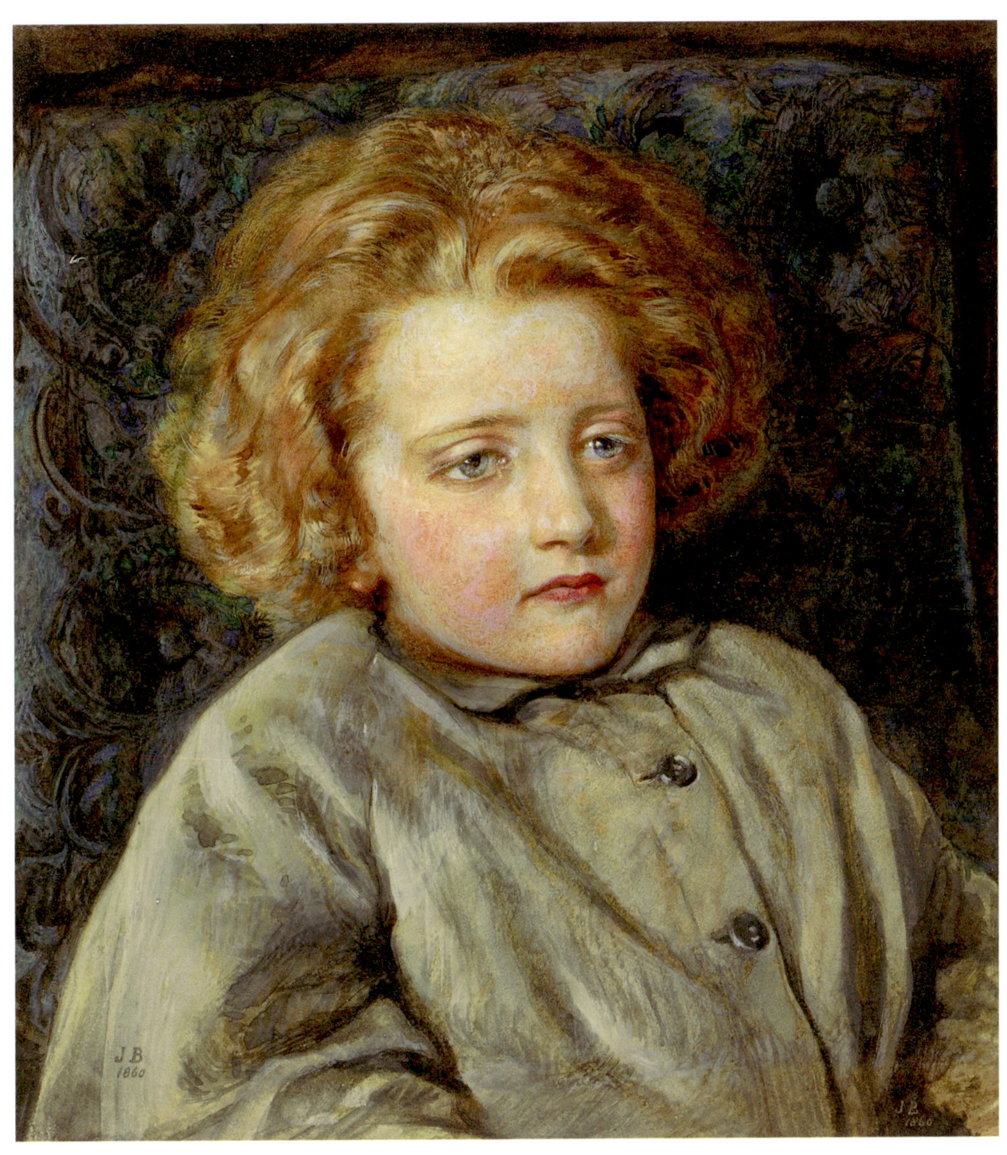
JB
1860
JB
1860

21 ***A Girl Sewing (Fanny Bell)*** **(1860)**

Pencil on paper
20.3 x 17.8 cms.
Inscribed: 'Decr 4. 1860' l.r.
Private collection

Judging from the date, and the resemblance to no. 22, the sitter for this beautifully finished drawing must have been Fanny Bell, who was staying with John and Rosa at Old Milverton, near Warwick, in December 1860. This is one of a series of drawings Brett executed in 1859 and 1860 which show young women engaged in domestic activities, sewing, reading, or writing, in subtle lighting conditions. They conform to Coventry Patmore's idea of perfect womanly virtue, expressed in his poem *The Angel in the House* (Brett had received a copy of *Faithful for Ever*, the third part of the poem, in October 1860). It seems very likely that he was hoping to have them engraved, as periodical illustrations or perhaps for an illustrated edition of the poem. In such works Brett shows his admiration for Millais's finely detailed drawings of similar subjects, which were translated into wood engravings by Joseph Swain and the Dalziel brothers. At this stage in his career, Brett was hoping to become a figure painter rather than a pure landscapist, and this drawing is one of his most successful attempts at a full-length figure. CP

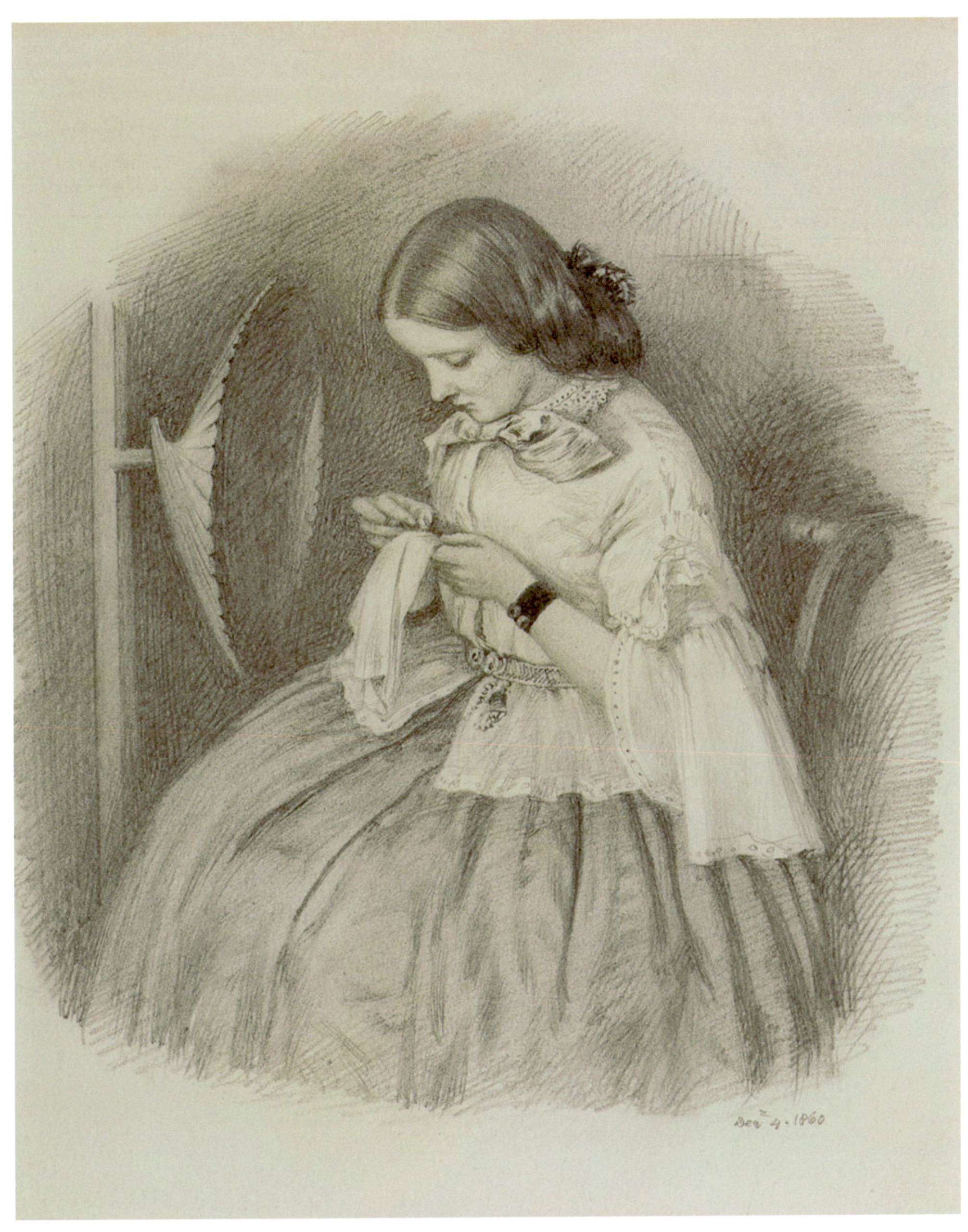
Decr 4. 1860

22 *Fanny Bell* (1860)

Pencil on paper
17 x 14.8 cms.
Inscribed: 'Dec 14 / 1860' l.r.
The Syndics of the Fitzwilliam Museum, Cambridge

Little is known about the sitter for this fine pencil portrait, Fanny Bell. She was evidently a childhood friend of John and Rosa because in October 1860 Brett records in his diary, after he had left Rosa on a visit to the Craggs at Coventry, 'Fanny Bell found! Hardly altered during the interval of 15 years' (JBD, 11 October 1860, p. 68). In 1845 Charles Curtis Brett's regiment was stationed at Coventry; John would have been 13 and Rosa 15. Fanny was presumably around the same age (Cordingly 1983, p. 6). In the November and December of 1860, John, Rosa and Fanny were all lodging together at Old Milverton, while John worked on his painting of *Warwick Castle* (untraced), and Rosa also made a portrait sketch of her (JBD, December 1860, p. 68; Sketchbook no. 7, PAF 8839). The alert expression of the sitter makes this one of Brett's most appealing portraits. Unlike many of his drawings of young women, there is no attempt to make her look alluring or modest: she stares straight ahead, suggesting a character that is self-confident and direct. CP

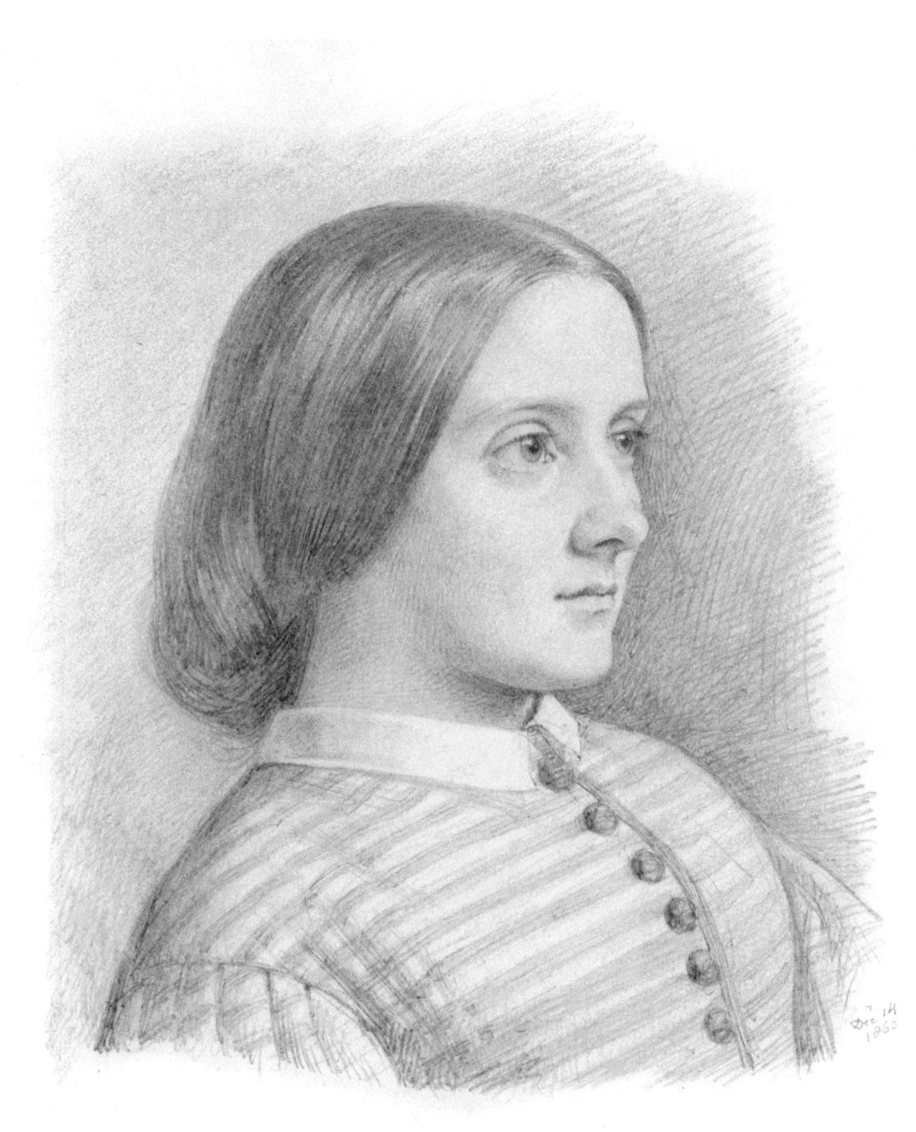

23 ***Rosa Brett* (1861)**

Pencil and white chalk on grey paper
25.4 x 16.5 cms.
Inscribed: 'march 12. 61' l.r.
Private collection

This portrait of Brett's sister Rosa (1829 - 1882) shows her as a modest character, the 'quiet nice girl' remarked on by Brett's friend Arthur Munby on a visit to his studio in 1865 (Munby MS, vol. xxxiii, 3 April). There is more than a hint of the constraints under which 19th-century women operated, especially those who had ambitions. It was considered unfeminine to put oneself forward, to 'make an exhibition' of oneself - and yet this is just what artists had to do, exposing their work, and, by implication, themselves to the public gaze and the possibility of disapproval. Rosa was a gifted artist: her best-known work, *The Hayloft* (1858, private collection) was exhibited under the pseudonym of 'Rosarius' at the Royal Academy, where it aroused enthusiastic critical notices in the press and private excitement amongst John Brett's Pre-Raphaelite friends. However, as the only daughter in a family of five children, it was perhaps inevitable that she should give much of her time to domestic duties, doing housework and teaching her younger brothers. She also suffered from ill health of an unspecified nature. CP

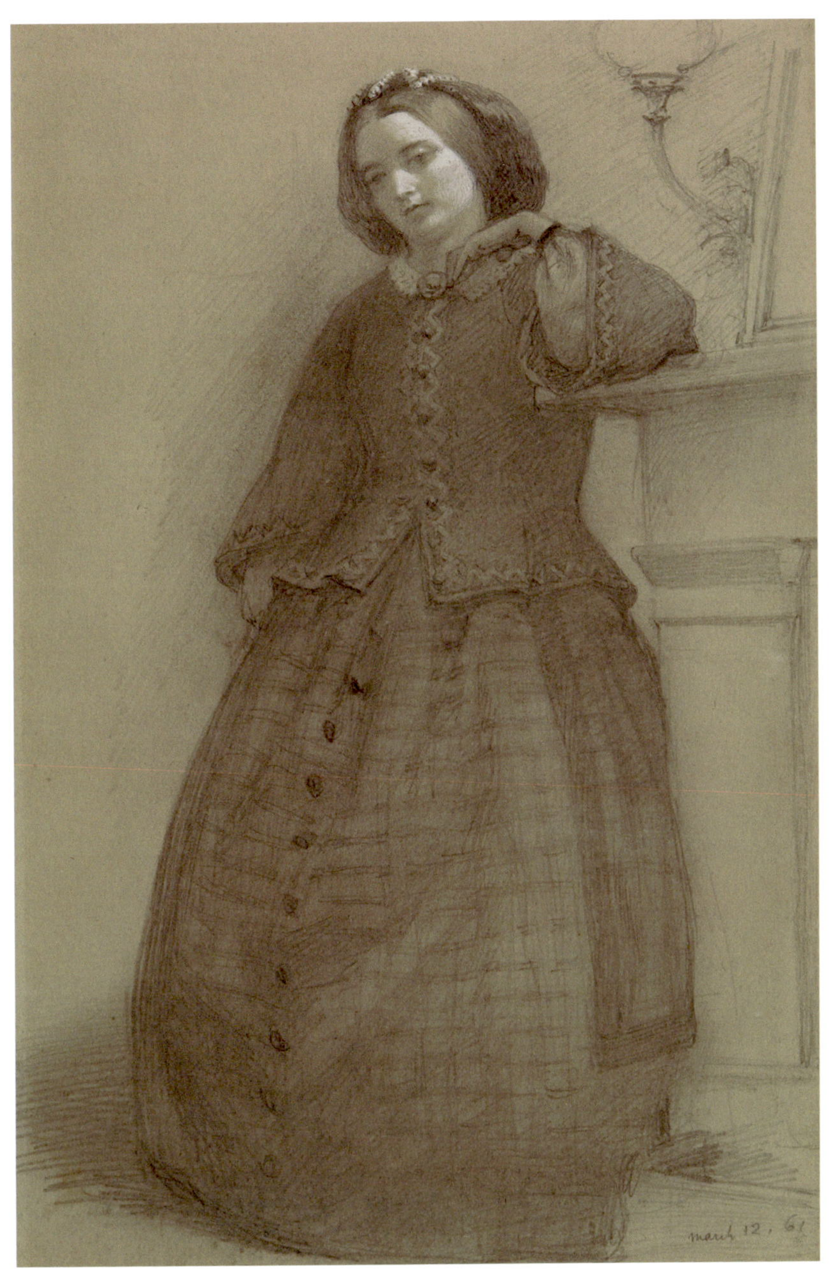
march 12, 61

24 ***Alexander Munro* (1861)**

Pencil on paper
19.5 x 14.5 cms. (oval)
Inscribed: 'J.B. / Florence / Decr 6. 61' l.l.
Private collection

Alexander Munro (1825 - 1871) was a sculptor whom Brett probably met through Rossetti in the early 1850s, or perhaps through Arthur Hughes, with whom Munro shared a studio between 1852 and 1858. Brett and Munro seem to have become quite close. In his diary, on 3 September 1860, Brett simply records 'Munro here', implying that he was visiting the artist at Old Milverton, where Brett was staying to work on his painting, *Warwick Castle* (JBD, p. 67). In 1862 and 1863, Munby twice records meeting Brett at 'one of Munro's pleasant gatherings' (Munby MS, vol. xiii, 24 June 1862; vol. xix, 17 June 1863). In December 1861, when this drawing was made, Brett was staying in Florence on his first visit to Italy, while Munro was there on honeymoon with his new wife. In a letter to his sister, dated 1 December 1861, he wrote 'Brett is here - we see each other every day'. Munro, like Brett's friend Thomas Woolner, made many portrait medallions, often showing the sitter in profile. Brett's drawing mimics this format, but it was a commission with a practical purpose. A few weeks later, in Rome, Munro had a cameo portrait of himself made for his sister and, he added, 'Brett made a good drawing of my profile at Florence for it' (letters in a private collection). CP

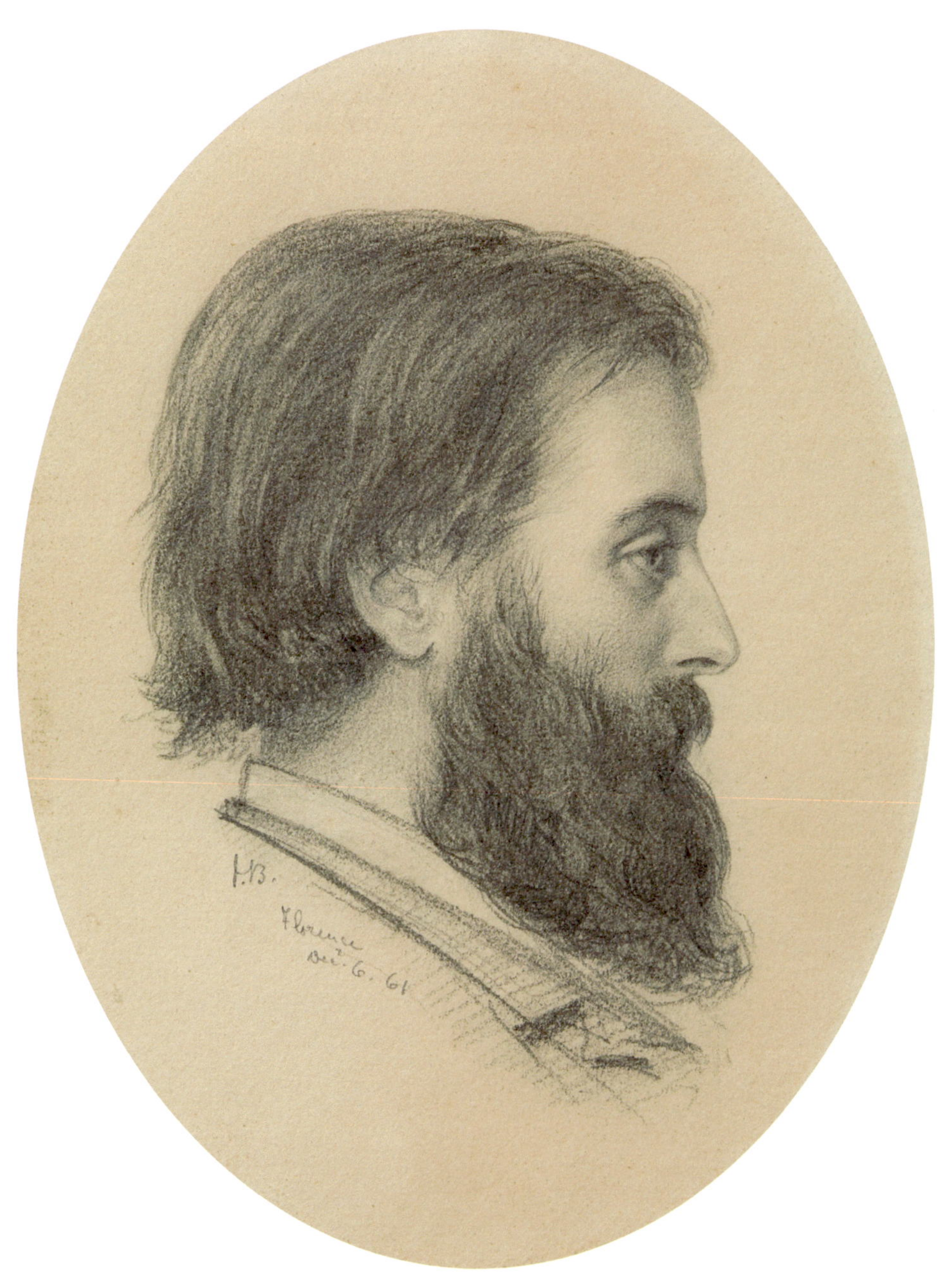
H.B.
Florence
Decr 6. 61

25 *Rosa Brett* (1862)

Pencil on paper

15.2 x 10 cms.

Inscribed: 'Canterbury. May 15. 1862' l.r.

Private collection

This spirited portrait suggests another side to Rosa's personality, in contrast to the restrained modesty of the full-length drawing of 1861. Here, she looks more like the sister whom John Brett described in 1858 'as ardent impulsive and unbendable as usual' (JBD, 25 December, p. 64). Surviving letters by John to Rosa show that they had a very close relationship (unfortunately, none of her correspondence to him has survived). In one letter, John refers to a family dispute over inheritance, and advises Rosa not to see her aunt Louisa in case she loses her temper: 'you had better avoid contact with L for fear of a rupture as I know you wd blow up & then all hope of getting what we want vanishes' (3 March 1854, private collection). In her own diary, too (1850-62, private collection), Rosa comes across as a forthright and feisty person, not at all the shrinking violet that was the Victorian ideal. CP

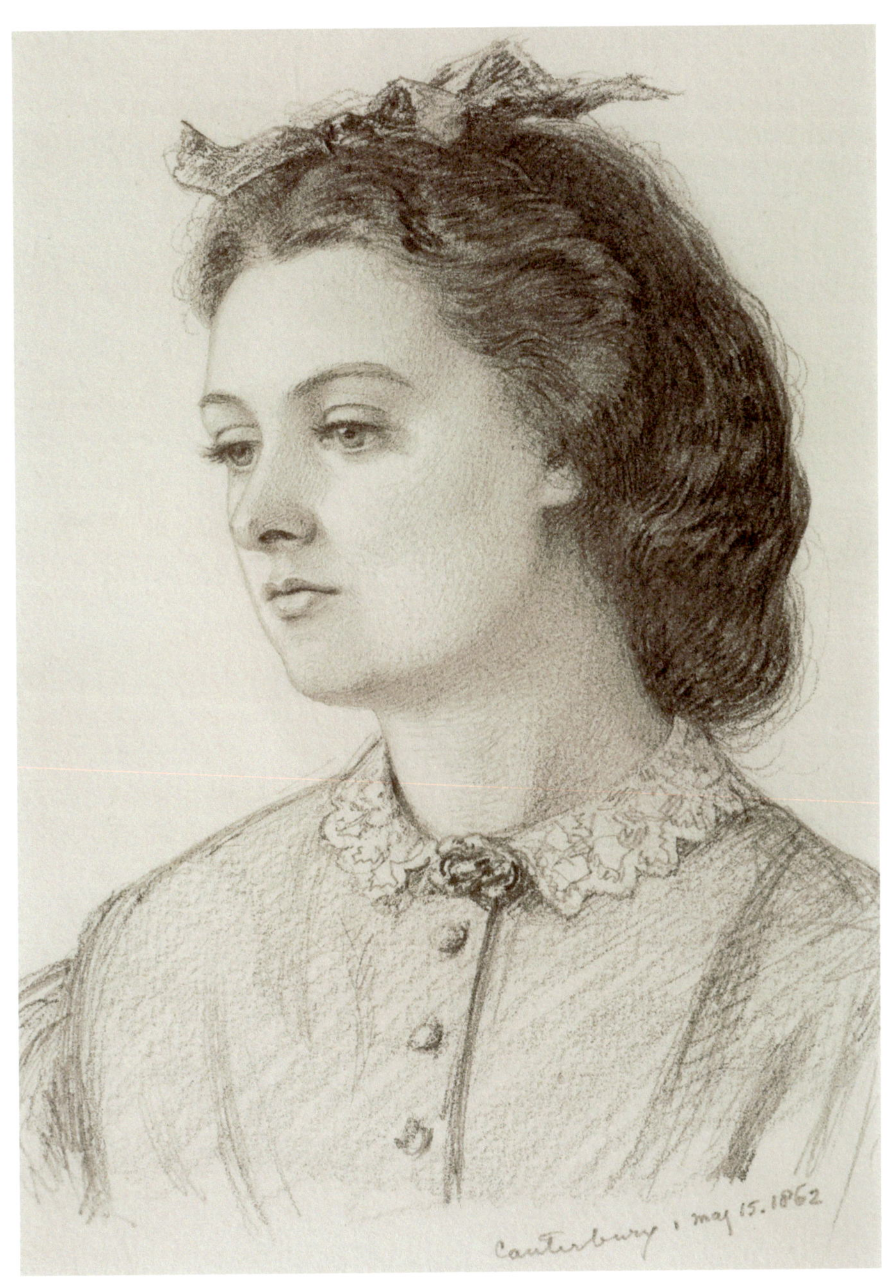
Canterbury : May 15. 1862

26 *Jeannette Loeser in Profile* (1863)

Pencil on paper
25 x 16.5 cms.
Inscribed: 'Florence / March 22. 63' l.l.
Private collection

This is the first known drawing by Brett of Jeannette Loeser, the companion of Jacques Blumenthal, who was to be the sitter for a full-length portrait, *Lady with a Dove* (no. 3). Over the next two years, Brett made many drawings of her. He was clearly entranced by her exotic beauty, with her dark, soulful eyes and luxuriant hair, which probably reminded him of Dante Gabriel Rossetti's drawings and paintings of Jane Morris. In this drawing he has chosen to show her finely chiselled profile against a dark background. She wears fashionable jewellery, as she does in the painted portrait. Brett was in Florence from December 1862 until April 1863, painting *Florence from Bellosguardo* (Tate Britain). While he was there, he became friendly with the international group which gathered at the house of Isabella Blagden, the friend of Robert Browning, and it is possible that he met Blumenthal and Madame Loeser there. He wrote to Jeannette on his return to England in April, and may have made arrangements to meet up again later in the year - there is a drawing of her in the sketchbook he used on board the SS *Scotia*, the ship that took him back to Italy (CCBD, 22 April 1863, p. 10; Sketchbook No. 13, PAF 8980). CP

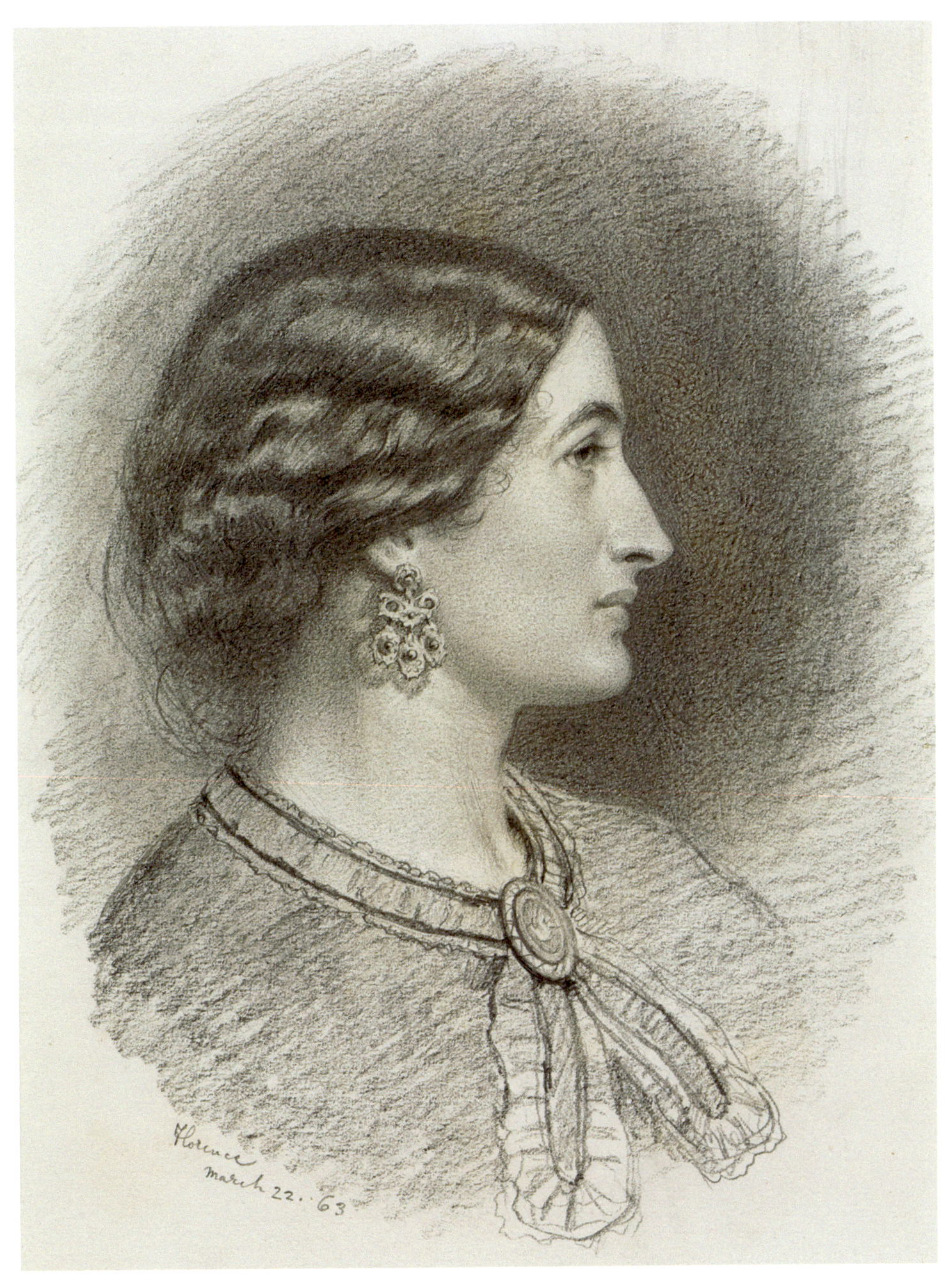
Florence
march 22. 63

27 *Jacques Blumenthal* (1863)

Pencil on paper
25.4 x 17.8 cms.
Inscribed: 'J.B. / Aug 1863' l.r.
Private collection

Jacques (originally Jacob) Blumenthal (1829 - 1908) was a musician who established himself as a fashionable pianist in court and aristocratic circles in London, after training in Vienna and Paris, which he left to escape the 1848 Revolution. He composed short piano pieces and songs which achieved wide popularity, and developed a successful international career as a recitalist, invariably returning to London for the season, where he presented an annual Grande Matinée Musicale in one of the great aristocratic houses. Brett probably met him in Florence in the spring of 1863, when he is first known to have made a drawing of Blumenthal's companion, Jeannette Loeser (no. 26). In August 1863, when this drawing was made, Brett was about to embark on the steamship SS *Scotia* to travel to Naples. The following year, Blumenthal encouraged Harry and Georgina Weldon to go to Capri, a place that was 'warm and cheap' (GWD, 9 December 1864, p. 2), and he may have done the same with Brett in 1863. Brett made a number of minutely finished drawings of Blumenthal in a sketchbook he was using in the winter of 1863-4 (Sketchbook no. 14, PAF 9009); perhaps these were studies for a painted portrait, or possibly Brett just found Blumenthal's face, with its dark, soulful eyes, an appealing subject for a drawing. CP

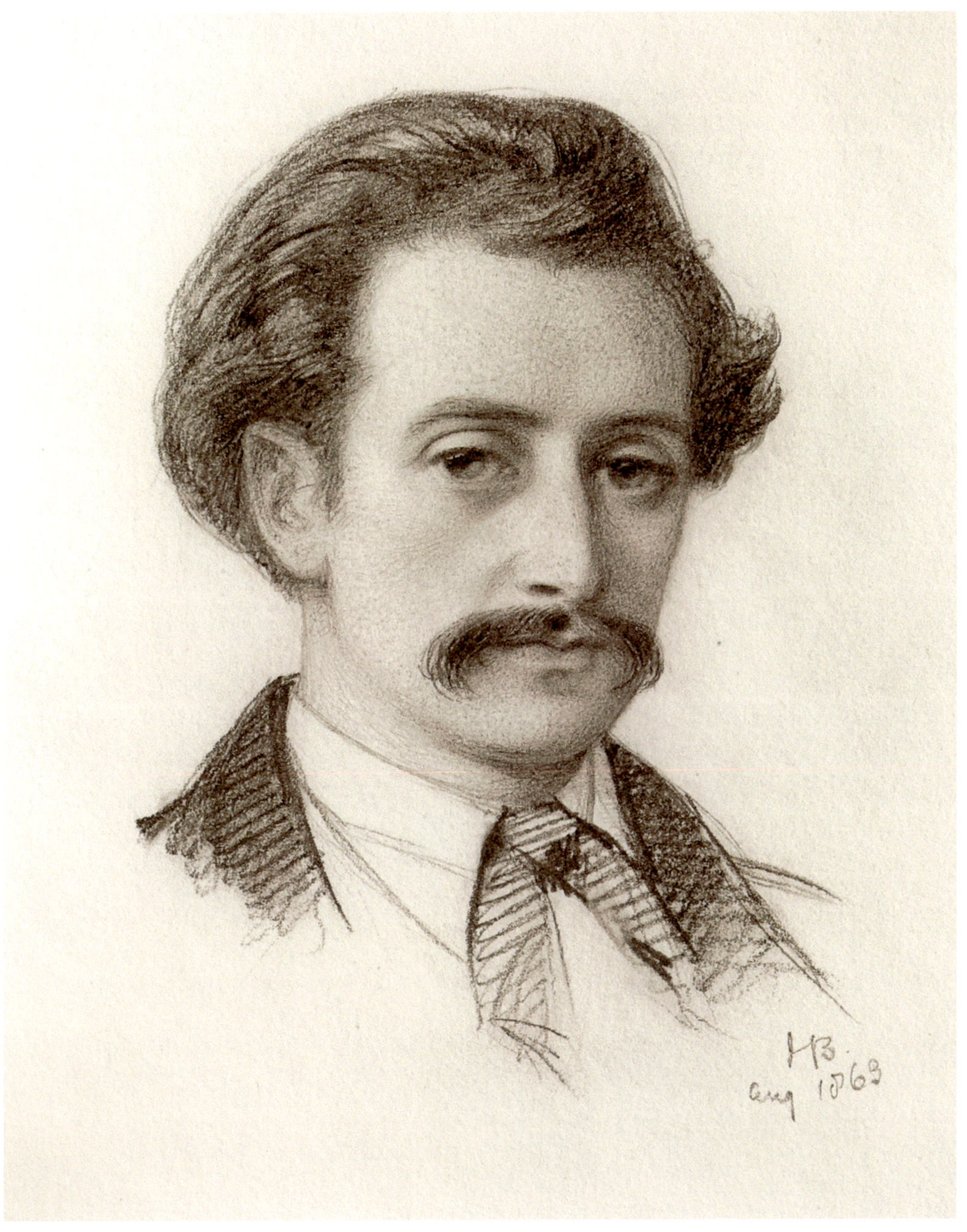
HB.
aug 1863

28 *Frances Martineau* (1865)

Pencil on paper
20.3 x 16.5 cms.
Inscribed: 'John Brett / Esher. June 27 / 1865' l.l.
Private collection

Frances Martineau (1839 - 1920), known as Fanny, was the wife of P. M. Martineau (1831 - 1911), a patron of Brett who became a family friend. He was a director of the sugar refiners David Martineau and Sons. In 1864 he commissioned Brett to paint two pictures of Morants Court, near Sevenoaks, Kent, a house which held personal memories for him, and the inscription he wrote on the back of one of the paintings describes Brett as 'my friend.' He remained on good terms with Brett, being invited to private views until the end of the artist's life, and in 1897 he provided Brett's daughter Pansy with her first commission as a bookbinder (Brett 2004, p. 6). Fanny married him in 1861 and bore him five children. Brett's drawing is one of his most successful works: her fine features and luxuriant hair are carefully delineated and her uplifted gaze suggests intelligence and spiritual wisdom. The drawing remained in Brett's possession. It is difficult to imagine why the Martineaus did not want to keep it unless the artist gave them a better one - or, perhaps, despite being a lovely drawing, it was not a good likeness. CP

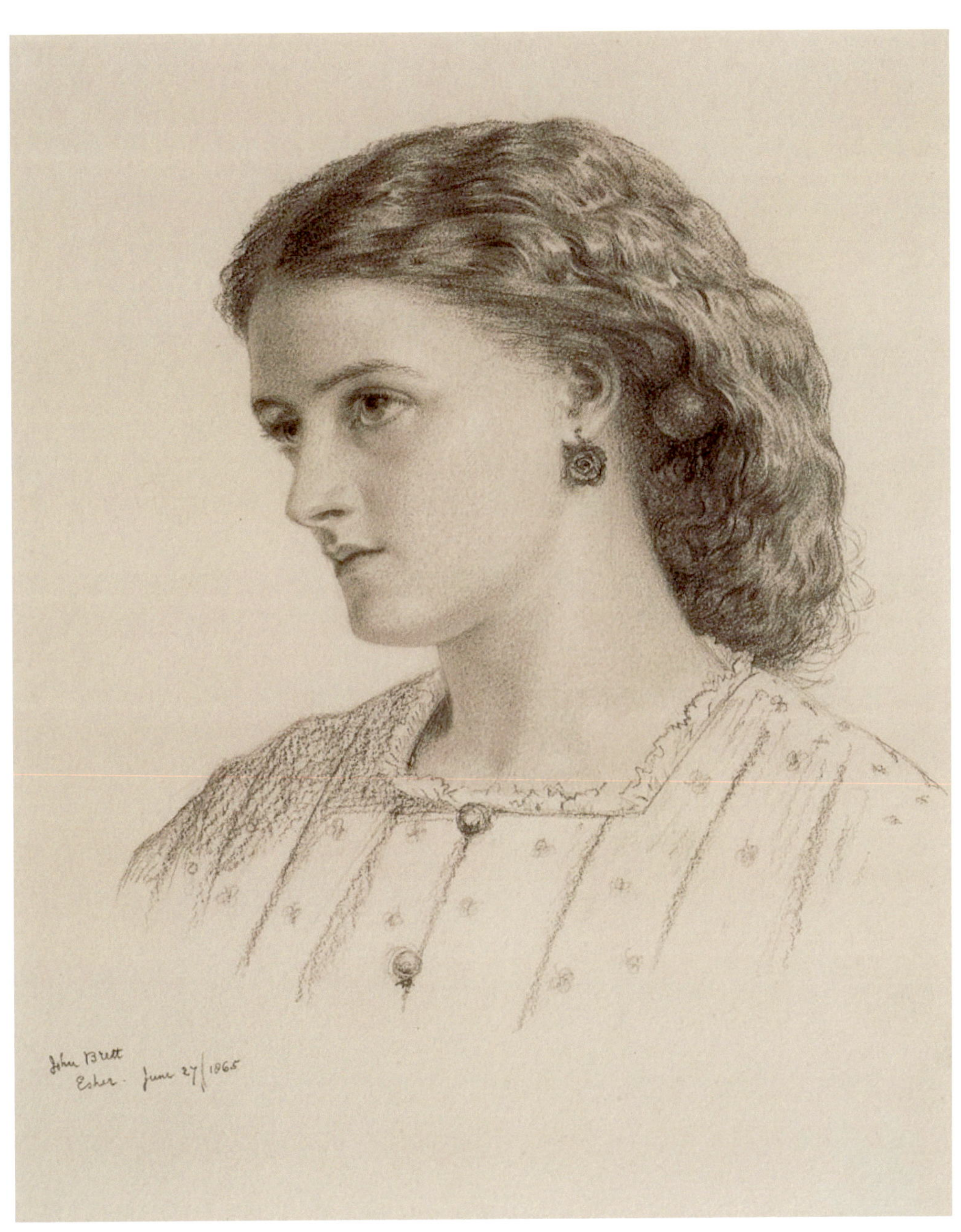
John Brett
Esher. June 27/1865

29 ***Georgina Weldon with her Dog* (1866)**

Pencil on paper

26 x 17.8 cms.

Inscribed: 'J.B. Sepr 1866' l.r.

Private collection

Georgina Weldon (1837 - 1914) was a singer whom Brett met in Capri in January 1865, soon after she had married Harry Weldon. The three became friends and saw each other regularly in the early spring of 1865, when Georgina apparently provoked the jealousy of Jeannette Loeser (GWD, 6 February 1865, p. 2). On their return to England, they corresponded, and Brett visited them at their house in Holyhead in Wales. They spent two consecutive Christmases together there, in 1866 and 1867, and on the second occasion Brett's sister Rosa and brother Edwin joined them. This is one of the many drawings Brett made of Georgina in the autumn and winter of 1866, when he was planning to paint her portrait. It was probably made early in September, before she had her hair cut, and just a few days after she had noted in her diary that Brett was inclined to fall in love with her (GWD, 29 August 1866, p. 5). Georgina's gaze does, indeed, suggest a coquettish intimacy, only slightly counterbalanced by the lively attitude of her pet dog, Dan Tucker, also known as Minkin (GWD, 9 December 1866, p. 6). The heads of both Georgina and her dog are drawn in very fine detail, while other parts of the drawing, particularly Georgina's hands, are much more sketchily indicated. CP

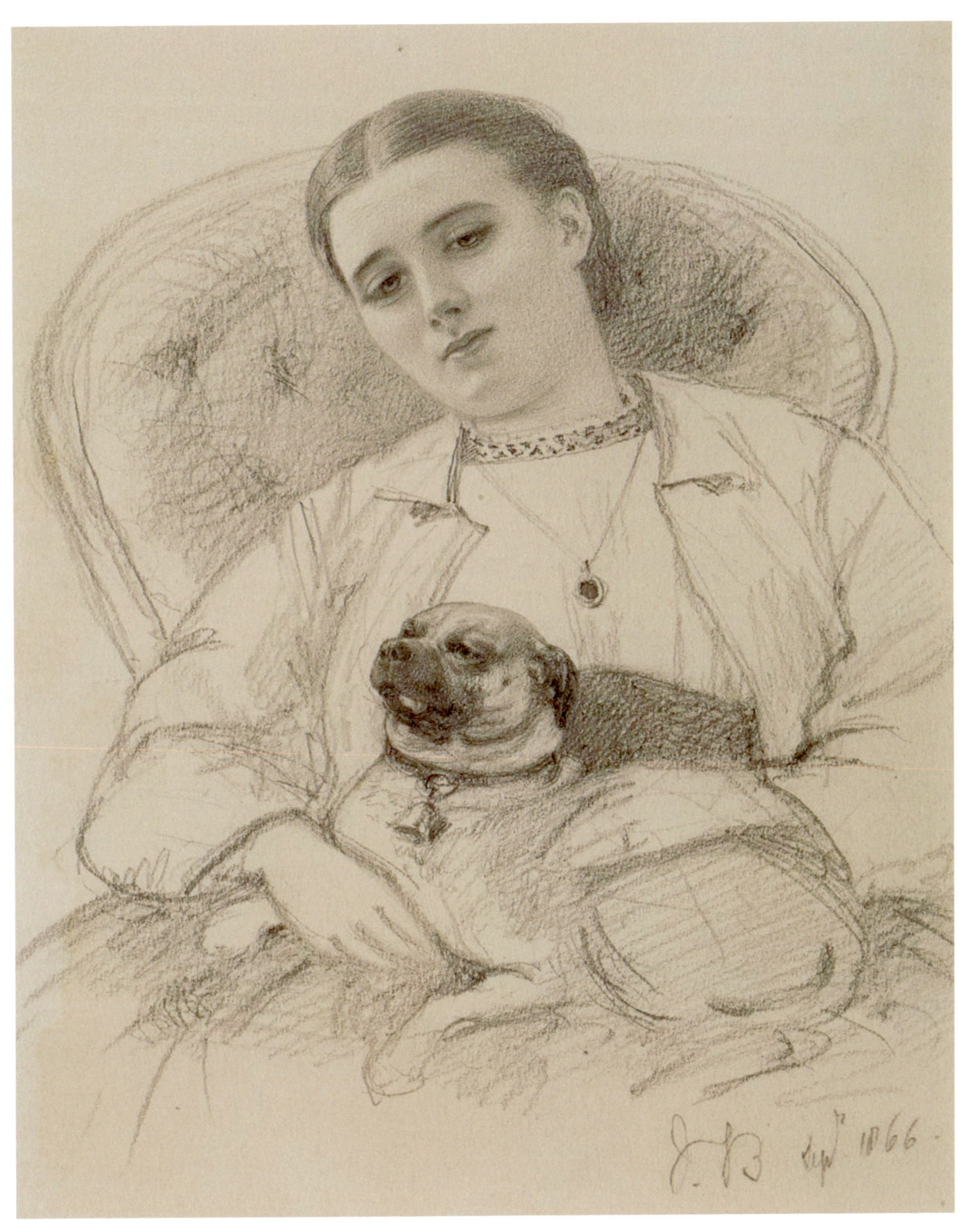

30 ***Sir George Young* (1868)**

Pencil on paper

25.3 x 20.3 cms.

Inscribed: 'april 14. 1868' l.r. and 'Drawn by John Brett at Formosa Cottage' (in another hand) l.c.

Private collection

Sir George Young, the third baronet (1837 - 1930), was a scholar of ancient Greek, best remembered for his translations of Sophocles's plays for the definitive Dover edition. He became a Fellow of Trinity College, Cambridge, in 1862, and he also trained as a barrister. In 1882 he was appointed a Church Commissioner. Young probably met Brett when the latter took lodgings at Pump Court, in the Temple, in 1860. Brett made two pencil portraits of Young, of which this one - made at his country residence, Formosa Cottage at Cookham, Berkshire - is the more successful. Like his portraits of Hughes and Blumenthal, this shows a man with dark, aquiline features, whose physiognomy and attitude suggest sensitivity rather than action. Young is portrayed as if deep in thought, as befits his scholarly career. Young was invited to Brett's private views in his studio in the 1870s, so he must have remained a good friend. CP

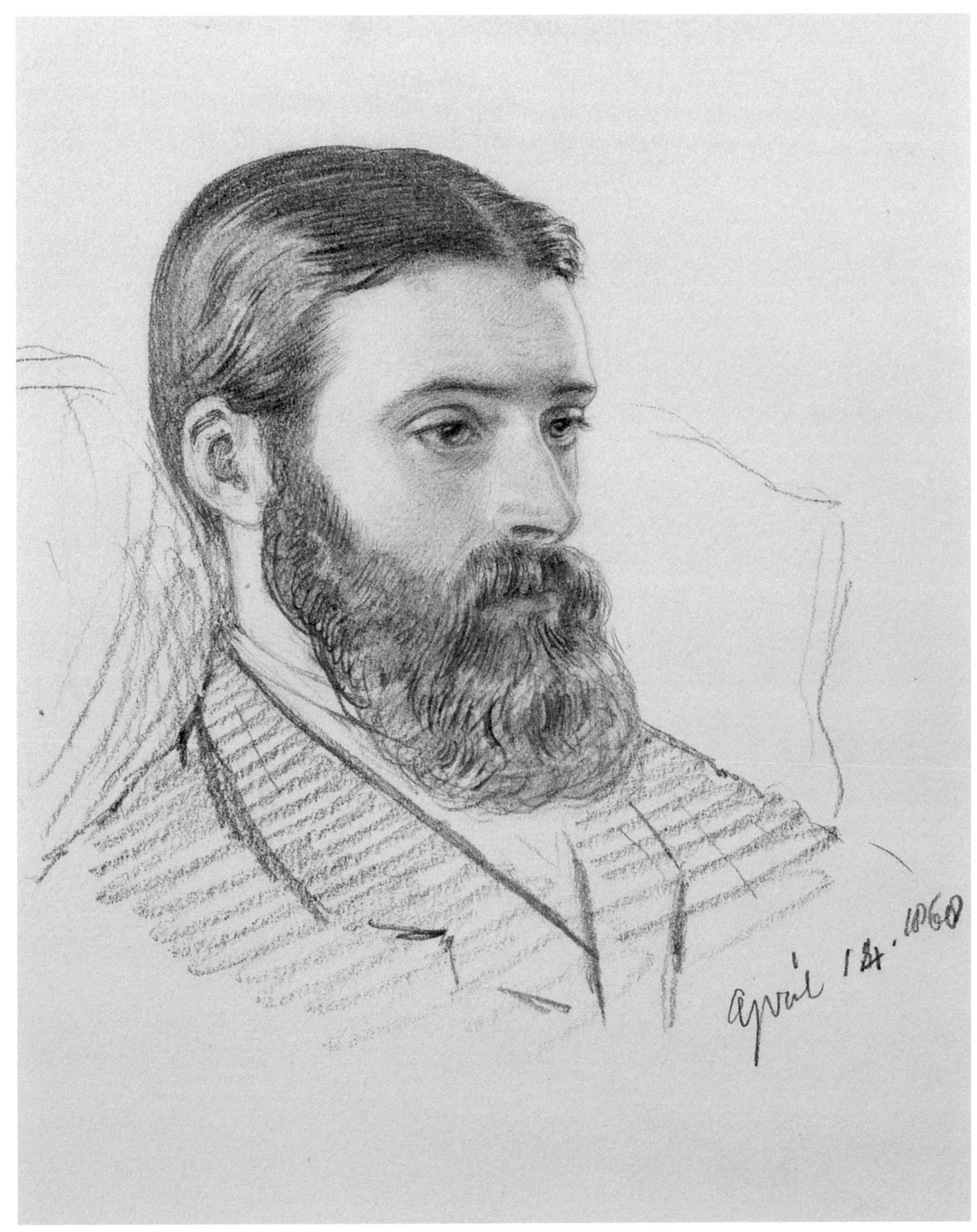

31 ***Profile Portrait of an Unidentified Woman ('Nance'?)* (1868)**

Pencil on paper
27.1 x 19.1 cms.
Inscribed: 'April 19. 1868' l.l. and 'm' l.r.
The Trustees of The British Museum, London

Until recently, the sitter for this drawing has been identified as Georgina Weldon. However, a comparison with other drawings of Georgina, particularly the fine drawing of her in profile (fig. 10), makes it clear that this cannot be correct. In one of Brett's sketchbooks there are four drawings, one of them dated 20 October 1867, which show a young girl with very similar features, drawn in informal poses and with her long hair flowing loose (Sketchbook no. 25, PAF 9292-5). A drawing from the previous year, made on St Valentine's Day, which seems to show the same sitter is inscribed 'Nance' (Sketchbook no. 18, PAF 9098). It may be hypothesised, therefore, that the sitter for this drawing was a girl named Nancy or Anne, with whom Brett was romantically linked. Although the sitter is not conventionally beautiful, Brett's economy of line and mastery of technique make this a most attractive work. He has rubbed the pencil to make an overall tint on the flesh and hair, so that the effect is closer to wash, and he has then superimposed rougher strokes over this tint. The sketchy handling of the clothing adds to the miraculous effect of the face, as if it were 'breathed on' to the paper. The drawing remained in Brett's possession. CP

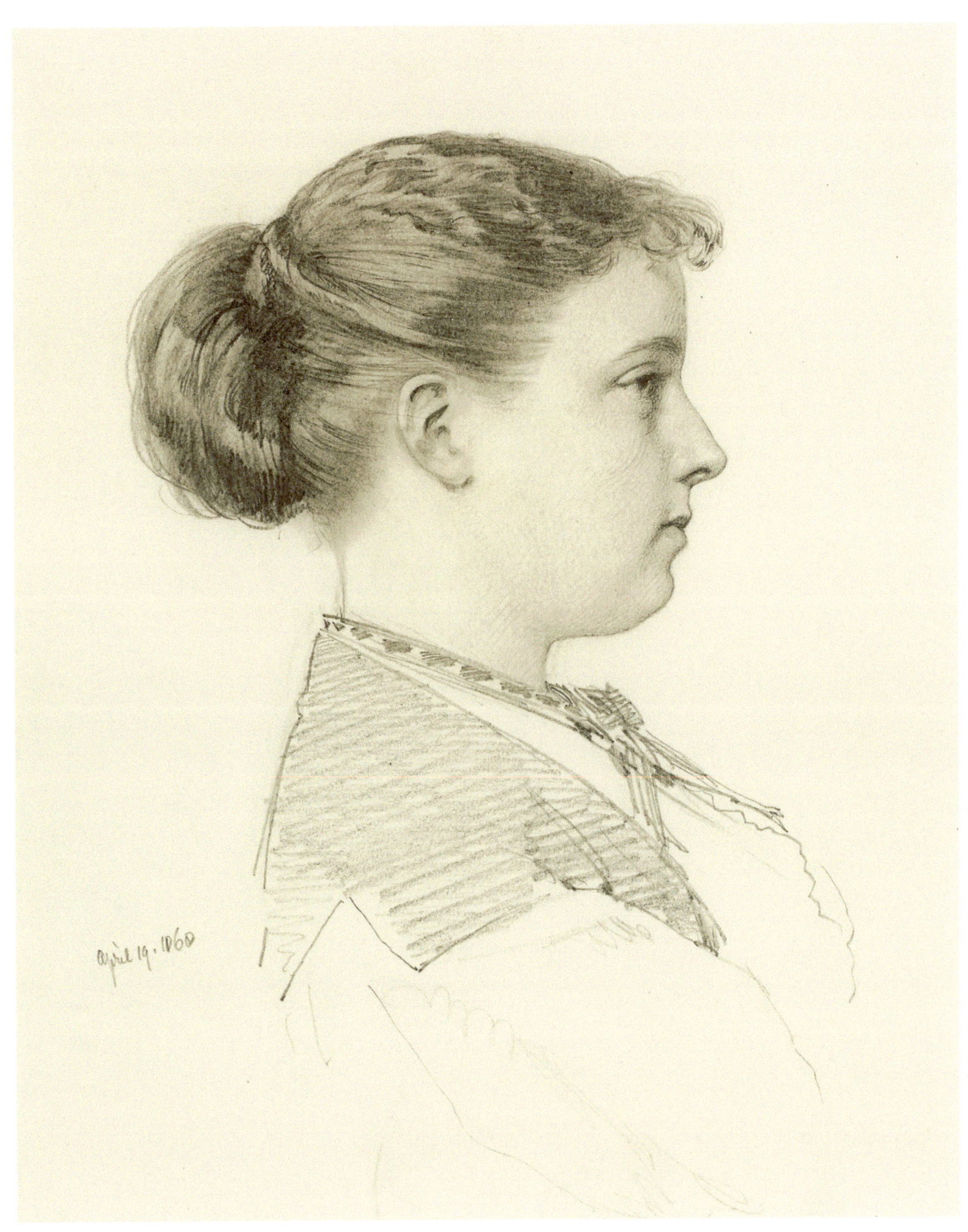
april 19. 1868

32 *Mrs Alfred Morrison* (1868)

Pencil on paper
33 x 25 cms.
Inscribed: 'Mrs Alfred Morrison May 68' l.r.
Private collection

Brett executed several portraits of Mrs Alfred Morrison. In July 1868 he sent her husband a receipt for £128, for an oil portrait and two pencil heads of Mrs Morrison and an etching of Mr Morrison, though none of these appears to have survived (fig. 31). This drawing was not one of those commissioned, since it remained in Brett's possession. Mabel Chermside, the daughter of a local rector, was 18 when she married the 44-year-old Alfred Morrison in 1866. She apparently enjoyed collecting exotic headdresses, like the one she wears in this drawing, from the places she visited. In the first years of her marriage she suffered two bereavements, losing a ten-month-old daughter and also her father, which may help to explain the wistful expression on her face. When Brett made this drawing she must have been heavily pregnant, for she gave birth to a son on 8 June 1868 (Dakers 2010). After her husband died in 1897, Mabel sold all his contemporary paintings, including those by Brett, and it is possible that she disposed of Brett's portraits of herself at the same time. CP

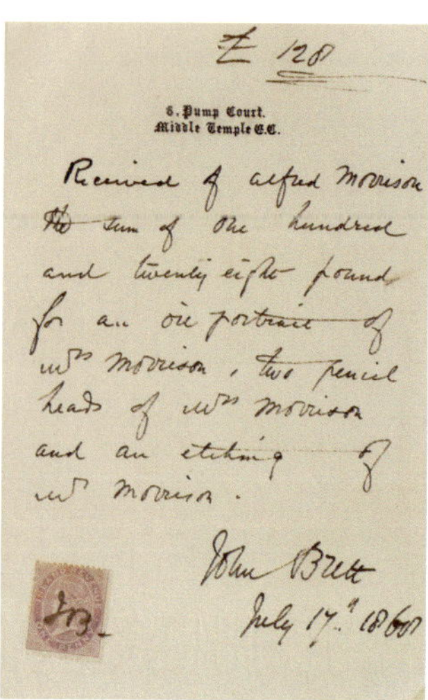

£ 128

6. Pump Court.
Middle Temple E.C.

Received of Alfred Morrison the sum of one hundred and twenty eight pounds for an oil portrait of Mrs Morrison, two pencil heads of Mrs Morrison and an etching of Mr Morrison.

John Brett
July 17th 1868

Fig. 31 ***Receipt for Portraits of Mrs Morrison***
17 July 1868
Lord Margadale of Islay

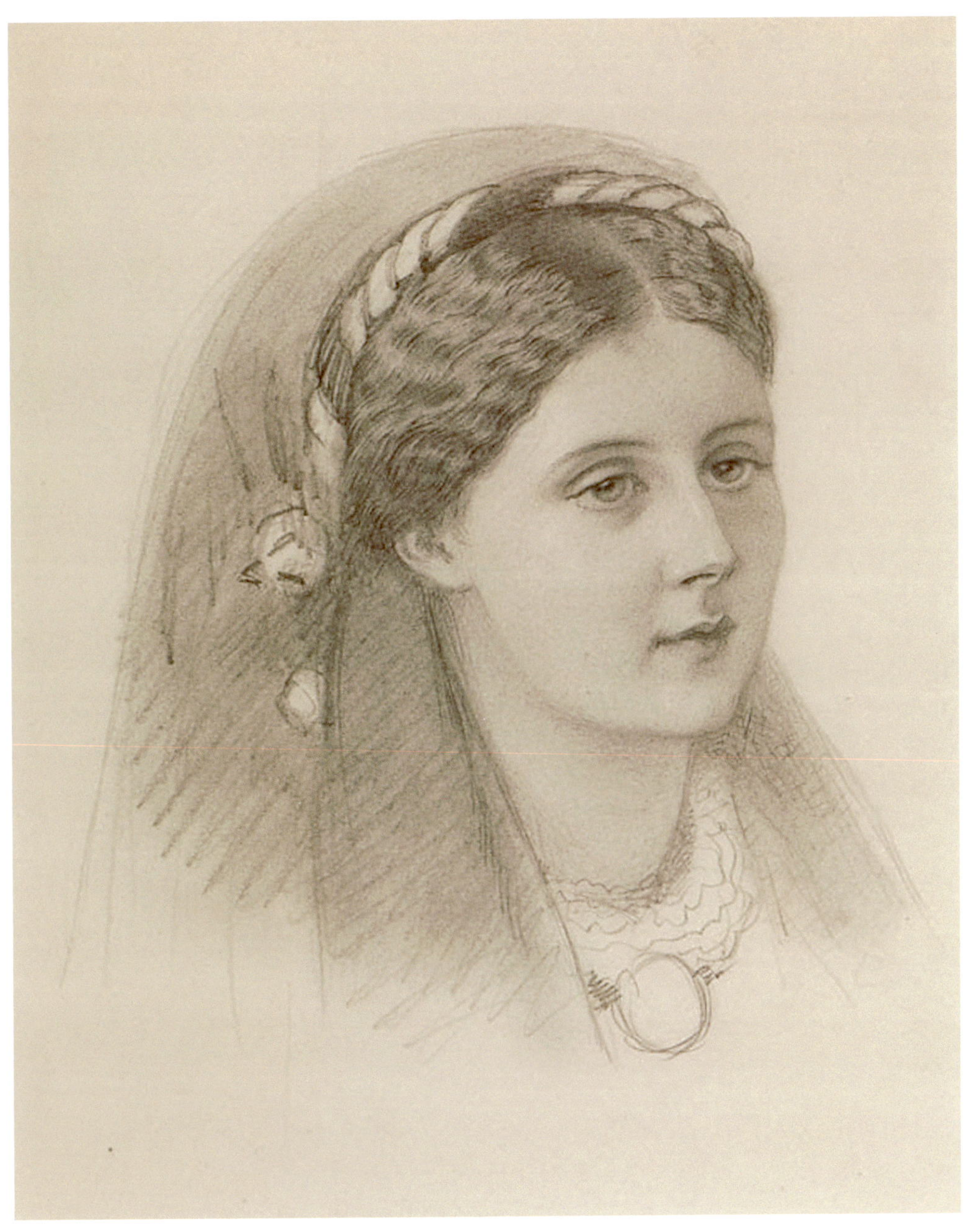

33 ***Alfred Morrison* (1870)**

Pencil, chalk and watercolour on paper
58.4 x 48.2 cms.
Inscribed: 'J. Brett / June 1870' l.l.
Lord Margadale of Islay

Alfred Morrison played a crucial role in Brett's life. He was an immensely rich collector, who shared Brett's interests in boats and the sea, and in the 1860s his commissions and purchases enabled Brett to embark on a series of large seascapes, establishing the pattern of work that would sustain him for the rest of his career. He also bought *The River Dart* (no. 38) and *Lady with a Dove* (no. 3). Surviving letters in the Morrison archives show how much Brett appreciated his patronage. In this portrait, the use of watercolour gives a lifelike colour to the flesh and lips, but we are given few clues to Morrison's personality. According to his obituary, Morrison was a man of 'fastidious taste [and] retiring disposition', and the impression Brett gives of him is that he was both reticent and somewhat disdainful (*The Times*, 27 December 1897, cited Dakers 2010). His first major collection was of portraits of famous men and women - in less than ten years he amassed 3,000 engraved portraits and this may well have been linked to his desire for status and pedigree. He was the son of a self-made man, James Morrison. CP

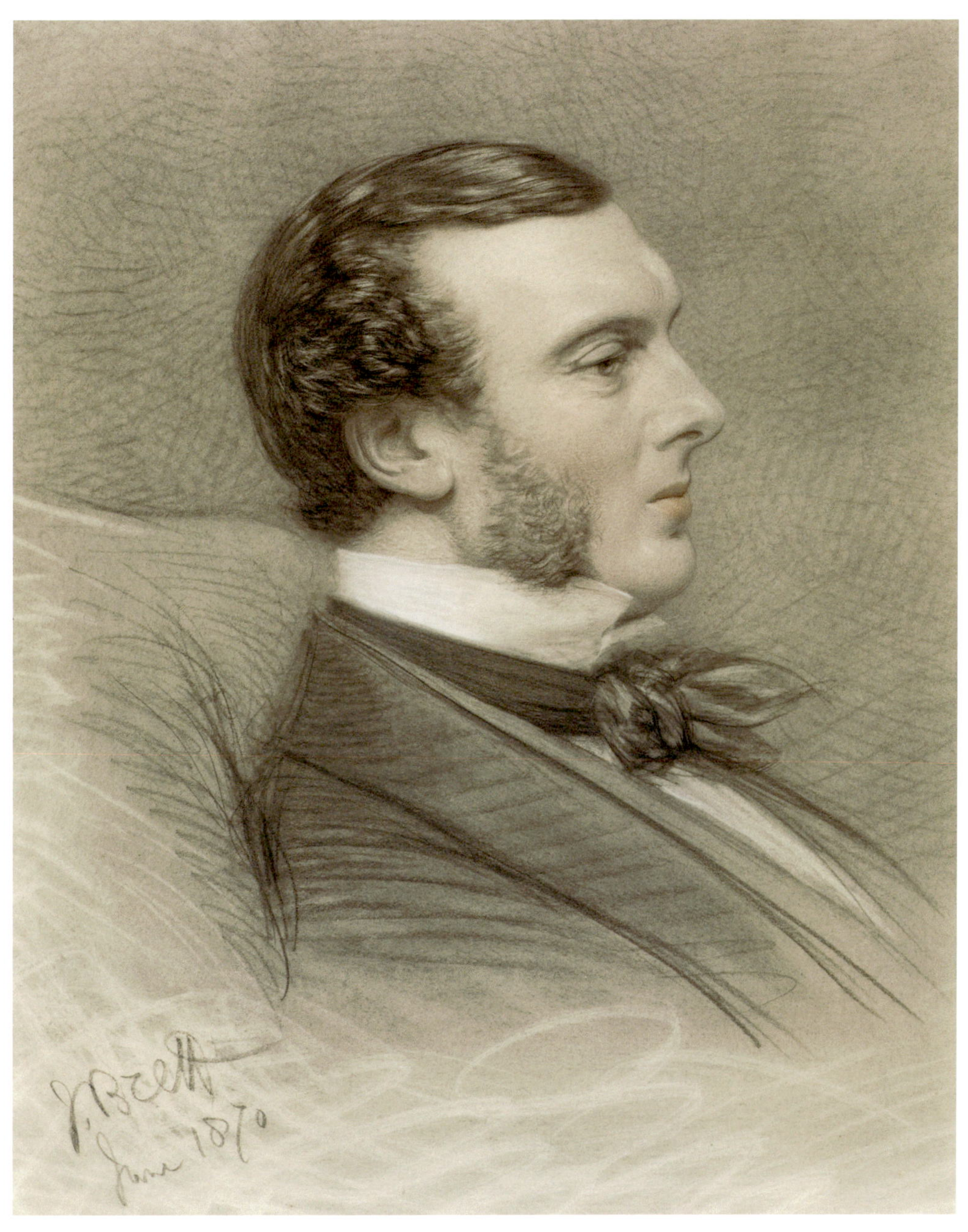

34 *Mary Brett* (about 1870)

Pencil on paper
16.2 x 10.3 cms.
Private collection

Rather surprisingly, Brett is not known to have made any detailed drawings of Mary Ann Howcroft, who became his common-law wife, at least, in the summer of 1870 (see no. 5). There are several studies of her in his sketchbooks, but they are all rapidly executed, often made when she was busy looking after the children. After 1870, all Brett's known portraits, whether drawings or oil paintings, are of his own family: he seems to have abandoned his earlier practice of making meticulously detailed portrait studies of friends and patrons. Perhaps this was simply because of the pressures on his time. In the 1870s he was increasingly interested in astronomy, and took an active part in the proceedings of the Royal Astronomical Society. He also designed two houses for his family, both of them built by the Birmingham firm of architects, William Martin and John Henry Chamberlain. These activities, combined with the necessity of producing plenty of saleable paintings and bringing up seven children, left Brett with little spare time. CP

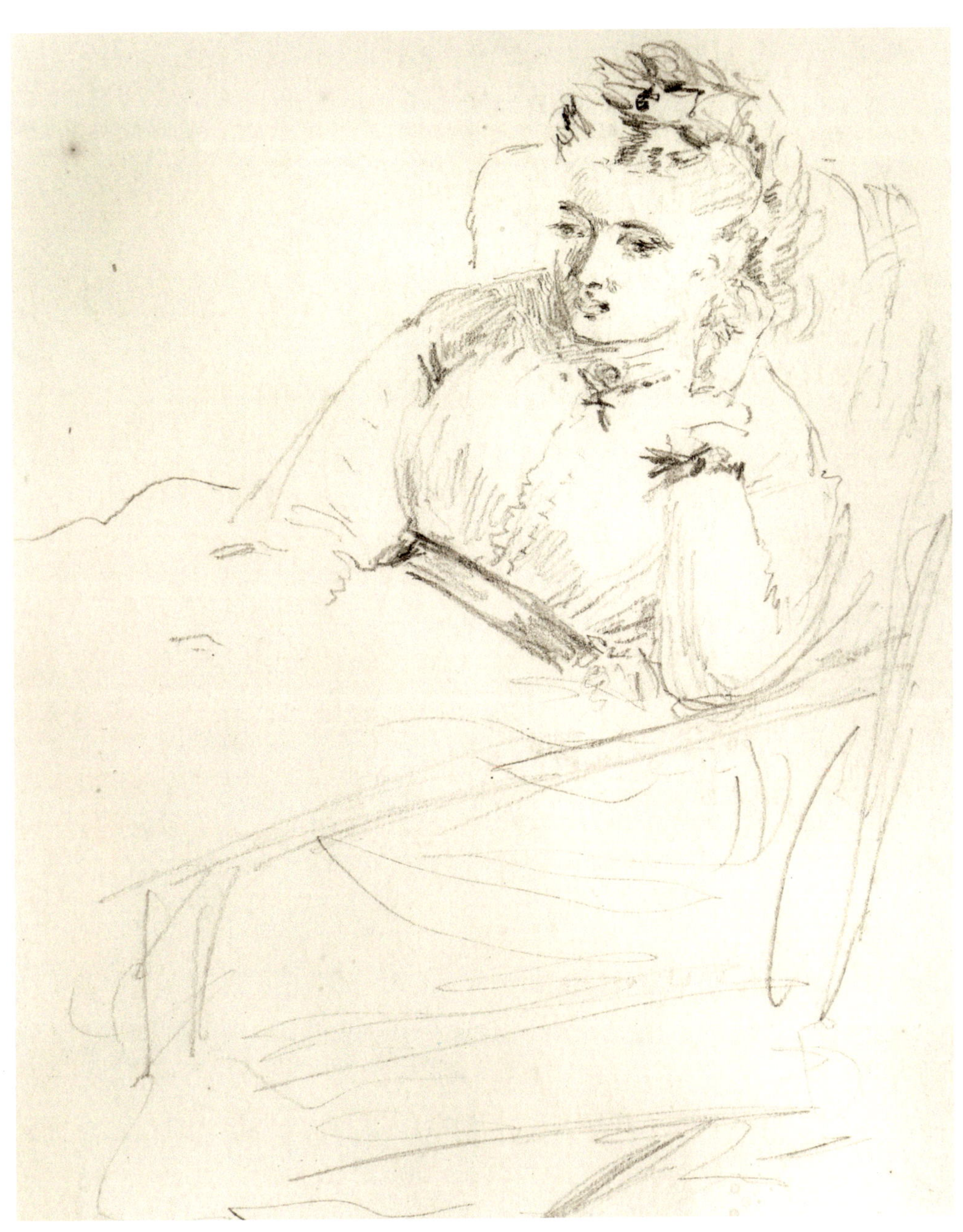

Sketchbooks

There are 72 sketchbooks by John Brett in the collection of the National Maritime Museum. Most of the drawings are of landscape subjects, though there are also a number of fine portraits.

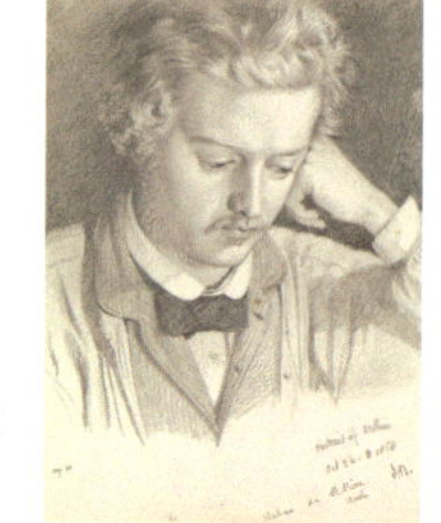

35 ***Arthur Brett (1858)*** From Sketchbook no. 5 (PAF 8777)
Pencil on paper 17.6 x 12.5 cms.
Inscribed: 'Portrait of Arthur / Oct 26. 1858 / Château de St Pierre J.B.' and 'age 20'. National Maritime Museum, Greenwich, London

This beautiful example was made while Arthur was staying with Brett at the Château de St Pierre, his base while he worked on the *Val d'Aosta* (fig. 2). Brett wrote much later, in notes for a lecture, that 'a happy expression on the human face is largely dependent on reflected light' and he added that people look their best at the dinner table, when light reflected from the white tablecloth gives them 'a more or less angelic appearance' (Brett 1892, pp. 16, 44-5). CP

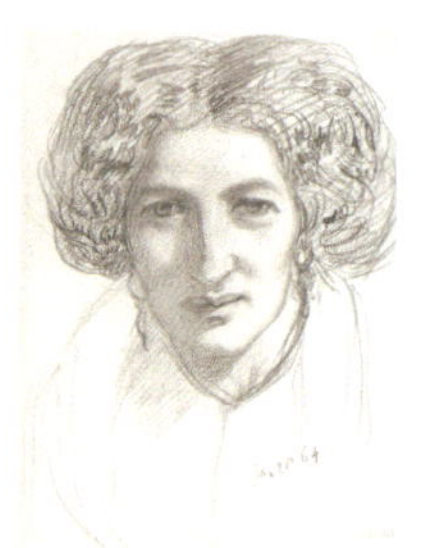

36 ***Jeannette Loeser (1864)*** From Sketchbook no. 14 (PAF 9009)
Pencil on paper 25.7 x 17.6 cms.
Inscribed: 'Jan 28 64'. National Maritime Museum, Greenwich, London

In this extraordinary drawing, which strongly suggests that Brett and Jeannette had an intimate relationship, Jeannette's face is studied as if it were a piece of sculpture, with a softness in the modelling which is reminiscent of Michelangelo's chalk drawings. CP

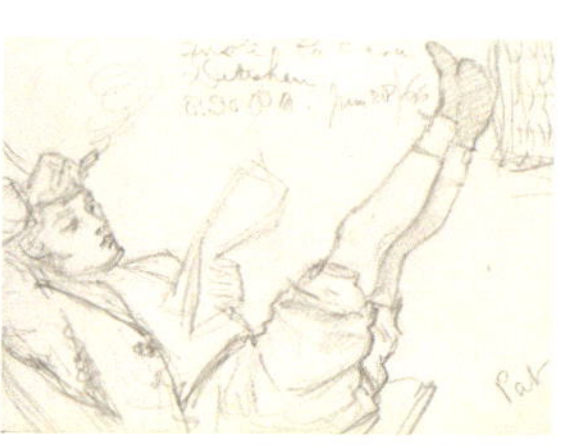

37 ***Edwin Brett (1866)*** From Sketchbook no. 20 (PAF 9165)
Pencil on paper 17.5 x 25.8 cms.
Inscribed: 'Fuori la casa [Outside the house] / Dittisham / 8.30 P.M. Jun 28 / 66' and 'Pat'. National Maritime Museum, Greenwich, London

Brett spent two or three months in Dittisham, Devon, in 1866, painting *The River Dart* (no. 38) in the open air, in the company of his brother Edwin, whose family nickname was Pat. This delightfully informal drawing was evidently made on a hot day which reminded Brett of his travels in the Mediterranean. CP

Landscapes

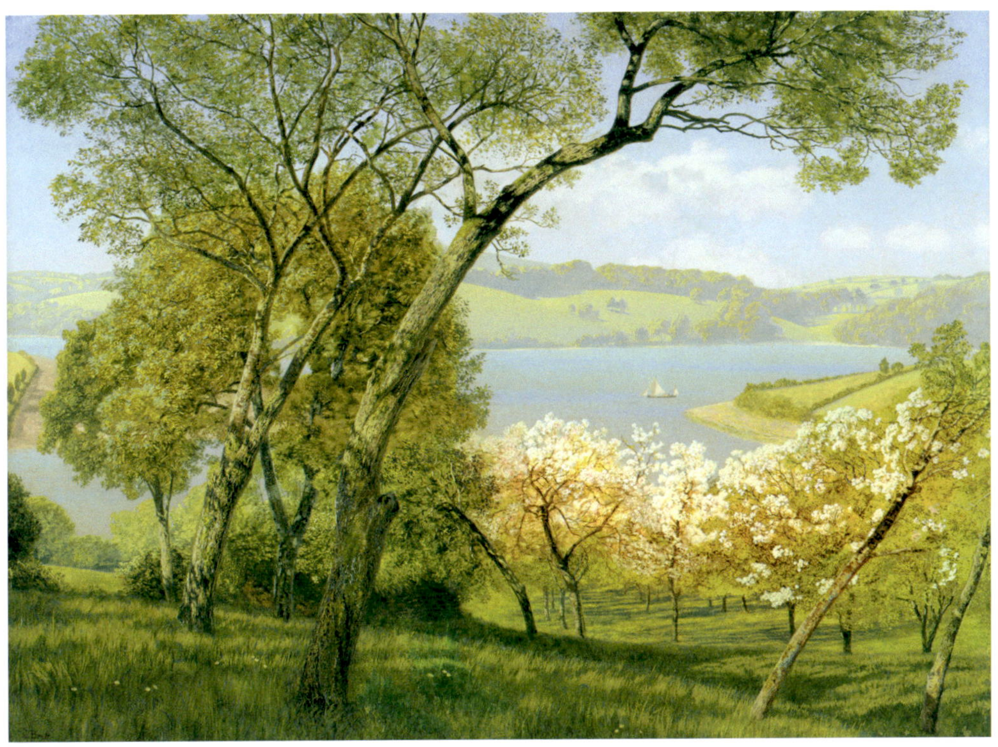

38 ***The River Dart* (1866)**
Oil on canvas 45.7 x 61 cms.
Inscribed: 'J. Brett' l.l.
Exhibited: Royal Manchester Institution, 1866, no. 195
The Andrew Brownsword Arts Foundation

In 1865 Brett acquired his own small yacht, the *Baby*, and sailed it around the Isle of Wight and as far as South Devon. In May, June and July 1866, he was based at the village of Dittisham, a few miles upriver from Dartmouth, and it was there that he painted *The River Dart*. He was kept company for some of the time by his brother Edwin and also by an attractive girl with dark eyes, who probably modelled for a figure that was originally inserted in the foreground of the painting, seated in the shade of the foremost tree. Brett's viewpoint was a little to the west of Dittisham, on the west side of the river. The view has changed little, although only a few plum trees remain of the orchards which once covered the hillside. The bend in the river to the right leads to the open sea at Dartmouth, and the solitary boat is an idealised portrait of the *Baby*. Soon after its completion, *The River Dart* was bought for £75 by Alfred Morrison, and Brett sent him a receipt on 22 August 1866. CP

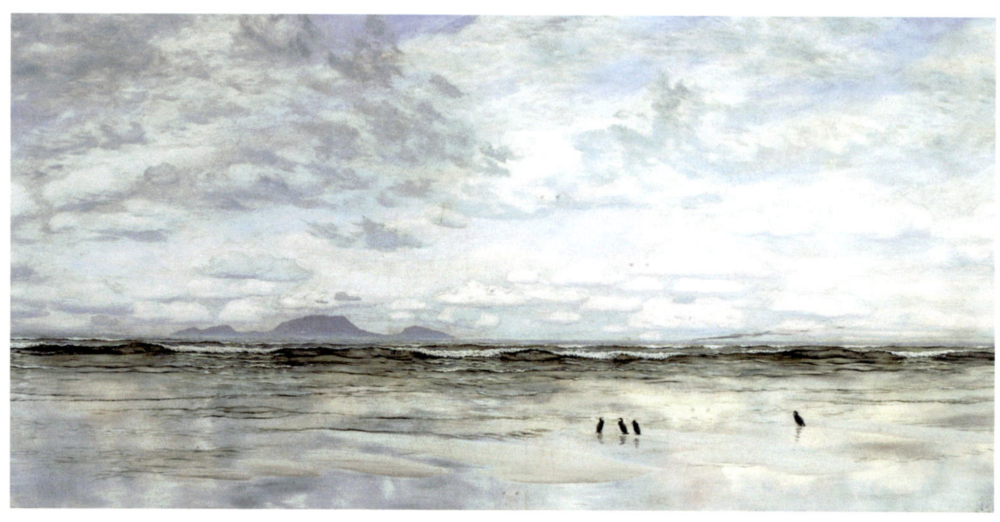

39 ***A Summer Day, South Wales, White Sands Bay*** **(1872)**

Oil on canvas 84 x 145 cms.

Inscribed: 'J. Brett 1872' l.l.

Exhibited: Royal Academy, 1872, no. 912

Private collection

This impressive seascape was produced by Brett following his visit to Pembrokeshire in 1871, with his partner Mary and their baby son Michael. The famous beach near St David's is today renowned as a surfing destination. Here, Brett shows a deserted scene with just a few cormorants in the foreground and a string of rocky outcrops, known as North Bishop, on the horizon. A vast cloudy sky is reflected in the wet sand below. Waves break on the shoreline, but there is no major swell. The work was exhibited at the Royal Academy in 1872, along with *The South Bishop Rock, Anticipations of a Wild Night*, which showed a view slightly south of Whitesands Bay. The critic F. G. Stephens commented that the pair were hung too high to be appreciated. Two years later, however, after coming into contact with Brett's work in Birmingham (see pages 34-5), the manufacturer William Kenrick purchased both paintings directly from the artist (family account book), paying £150 each and displaying them in his new home, The Grove, at Harborne built by J. H. Chamberlain, 1877-8, another Brett patron. AS

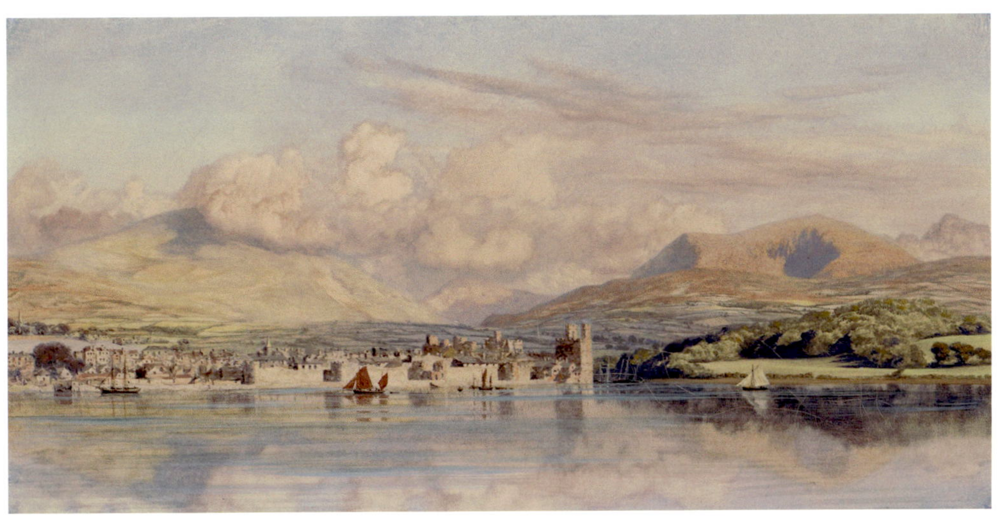

40 *Caernarvon* (1875)
Oil on canvas 24 x 47 cms.
Inscribed: 'Oct 1875' l.l.
Birmingham Museums & Art Gallery. Presented by Archibald S. Bennett, 1921

Brett shows the ancient Welsh town of Caernarfon, with its fortifications, from across the Menai Straits. The work was painted at the end of a three-month sojourn in Wales with his family during the summer and early autumn of 1875. Other related views and detailed atmospheric notes describing the scene appear in his sketchbooks of the time. The distinctive mass of Mynydd Mawr is obscured by wispy white clouds. The tide is in and the small trading and fishing vessels are accurately depicted. This surprisingly detailed study was purchased by the Birmingham architect J. H. Chamberlain in 1876 for £40. In early 1879 surviving correspondence reveals that Brett borrowed back the sketch to assist him in painting a much larger work, *The Stronghold of the Seison and the Camp of the Kittywake* (fig. 21) which was his Royal Academy painting that spring and came to the Royal Birmingham Society of Arts in the autumn, although it remained unsold. The larger work differs from this sketch in the formation of the clouds and the state of the tide, which is out (see pp. 32, 34). AS

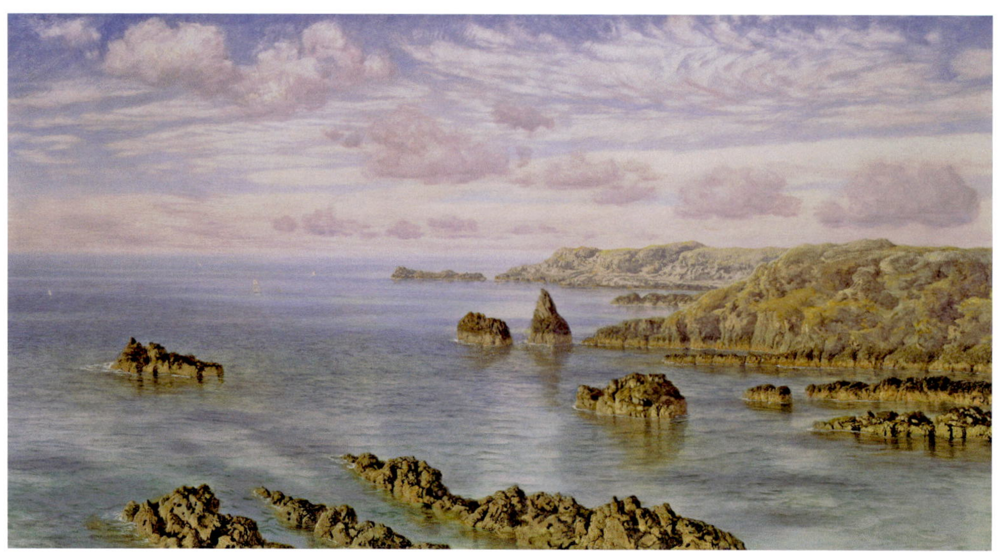

41 ***Southern Coast of Guernsey* (1875)**

Oil on canvas 61.2 x 108.2 cms.

Inscribed: 'Southern Coast of Guernsey from the Cliff over Moulin Huet / July 1875' (label on reverse)

Exhibited: RBSA, 1875, no. 361

Birmingham Museums & Art Gallery. Presented by the Council of Birmingham University, 1927

The Brett family visited Guernsey in 1874 travelling from Weymouth by GWR steamer on 6 July. They stayed at the Gardeners Royal Hotel, St Peter Port until mid-October (information supplied by Charles Brett) and Brett was particularly inspired by the east and south coast of the island. Twenty works were later inspired by his visit there. This particularly luminous and brilliantly coloured painting was exhibited at the RBSA as *On the Coast of Guernsey* at the Autumn Exhibition in 1875, already the property of Abraham Follett Osler, general manager of the famous glass-manufacturing company renowned for their cut-glass chandeliers. The work passed down through his family and was presented to the Council of the University of Birmingham by a Miss Osler in 1927, five years before the foundation of the Barber Institute of Fine Arts. Because of the lack of its own gallery, the University gifted it to the City Museum and Art Gallery. AS

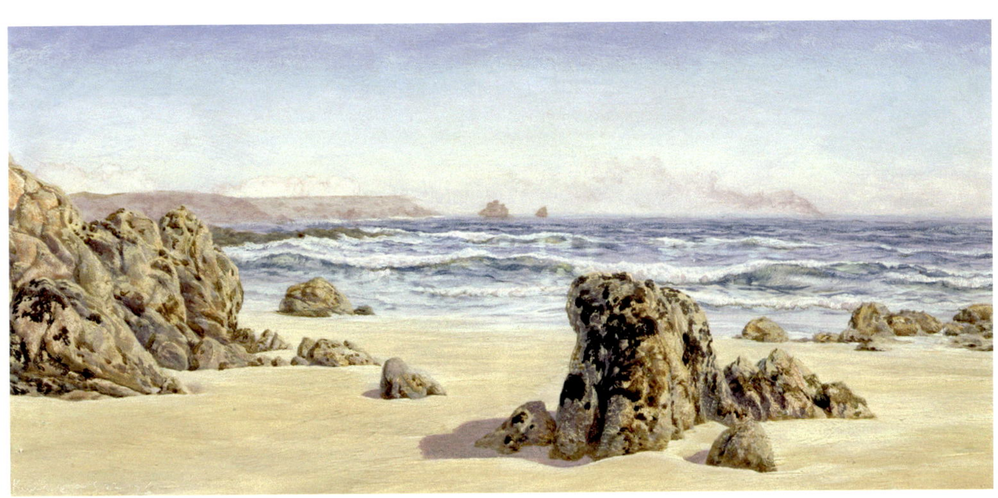

42 ***Kennack Sands* (1876)**

Oil on board 18 x 35 cms.

Inscribed: 'Kinnack Aug 22 / 76' l.l.

The Trustees of the Barber Institute of Fine Arts, University of Birmingham

This work is typical of the oil sketches Brett produced on the spot during his summer excursions to the seaside. He was in Cornwall in 1876 and his sketchbooks show him working on the Lizard peninsula. This view is taken from the western part of Kennack Sands, on the east side of the Lizard, looking in an easterly direction towards the distant Pedn Boar Point. The dark rocky outcrops in the middle distance are the Caerverracks. Brett would spend typically two or three hours on such a sketch, often recording the exact day of production in the inscription. The artist frequently slightly misspelt Cornish or Welsh place names as here. These 'on the spot' sketches were not intended for exhibition, although Brett did exhibit them in Birmingham in the spring exhibition, after some initial reservations, with considerable critical success (see p. 29). Sketches were often sold to patrons and framed accordingly - this work has an original Dolman frame. Brett sometimes borrowed back sketches and used them to inspire later paintings (see p. 113). This work is closely related to *These Yellow Sands* (private collection), a work exhibited by Brett in 1883 at the Royal Academy. This sketch was purchased by J. H. Chamberlain for £50 in 1877 (Penzance 2006, p. 86), the Birmingham architect who also owned *Caernarvon* (no. 40) and four other works by Brett. Although there is no documentary evidence, it is likely Brett borrowed back the sketch for inspiration. AS

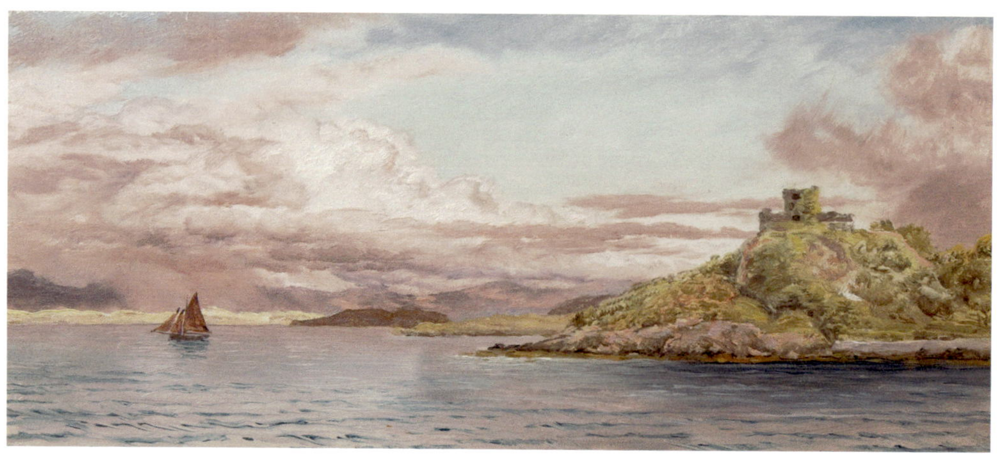

43 ***Dunollie Castle* (1885)**
Oil on canvas 18 x 35 cms.
Inscribed: 'Dunollie castle 3 Aug 85' u.l.
Exhibited: RBSA, 1887, no. 133
Private collection

This sketch shows the 12th-century castle, the former seat of the MacDougalls, the Lords of Lorne, which is situated on the northern side of Oban, Argyll, on the west coast of Scotland. Brett was in Scotland during the summer of 1885 and the following year mounted an exhibition of works at the Fine Art Society, London, *Three Months on the Scottish Coast*. In the accompanying catalogue essay he wrote that such sketches 'were ... produced in a single sitting, usually of two or three hours ... their shortcomings are often owing to the extreme haste occasioned by the pressure of unfavourable circumstances, such as cold, rain, wind or dust' (p. 7). The majority of the works Brett exhibited in Birmingham at the RBSA, and which were purchased by his local patrons, showed Welsh or Cornish views, but he did send several Scottish scenes. *Dunollie Castle* was exhibited in the Spring Exhibition in 1887 (no. 133, offered at £30), along with *Loch Nell Bay* (no. 123, offered at £40). The present work did not sell, although in the previous year in the Autumn Exhibition Sir John Holder, the brewer, had lent another Scottish view *An Argyll Eden* (see p. 34). AS

Bibliography/References

Anstruther 1992: Ian Anstruther, *Coventry Patmore's Angel: A Study of Coventry Patmore, his Wife Emily and 'The Angel in the House'*, London, 1992

Brett 1892: John Brett, 'Daylight in the Dwelling House', typescript, 1892, private collection

Brett 1899: John Brett, 'Realism in Painting', *The Contemporary Review*, no. 402, June 1899, pp. 823-30

Brett 2004: Charles Brett, 'John Brett and his Patrons', *The Review of the Pre-Raphaelite Society*, vol. xii, no. ii, Summer 2004, pp. 1-22

Cardiff 2001: David Cordingly, Christopher Newall, Ann Sumner, *John Brett: a Pre-Raphaelite on the Shores of Wales*, exhibition catalogue, National Museum & Gallery, Cardiff, 2001

CCBD: 'Charles Curtis Brett, Diary 1863-5', typescript, edited by Charles Brett (original in Brett family papers)

Cordingly 1983: David Cordingly, *The Life of John Brett, Painter of Pre-Raphaelite Landscapes and Seascapes*, PhD thesis, University of Sussex, 1983

Dakers 2010: Caroline Dakers, 'Alfred Morrison 1821-1897; "Victorian Maecenas"', chapter in forthcoming book

Davies 1985: Stuart Davies, *By the Gains of Industry: Birmingham Museums and Art Gallery, 1885-1985*, Birmingham, 1985

Dixon 2006: Carolyn Valentine Dixon, *Laura Theresa Epps - Lady Alma-Tadema, Artist (1852-1909)*, MPhil thesis, University of Sussex, 2006

ET: 'Memoranda of the Early Travels of our Children, written for them by John Brett and Mary Brett on alternate Sundays commencing in the Autumn of 1879 at Penally', typescript, edited by Charles Brett (original in Brett family papers)

Fredeman 1967: William E. Fredeman, ed., *A Pre-Raphaelite Gazette: The Penkill Letters of Arthur Hughes to William Bell Scott and Alice Boyd 1886-97*, Manchester, 1967

Funnell and Warner 1999: Peter Funnell, Malcolm Warner *et al.*, *Millais: Portraits*, exhibition catalogue, National Portrait Gallery, London, 1999

Gridley and Hickox 2001: Chris Gridley, Mike Hickox, unpublished paper given at a study day, National Museums and Galleries of Wales, Cardiff, 3 November 2001

GWD: 'Georgina Weldon, Diary 1864-71', typescript, edited by Charles Brett, extracts taken from the Treherne family MSS, by kind permission of Dr Joanna Martin

Haight 1978: Gordon S. Haight, *The George Eliot Letters*, New Haven and London, 1978

Hartnell 1996: Roy Hartnell, *Pre-Raphaelite Birmingham*, Studley, Warwickshire, 1996

Hickox 1985: Mike Hickox, 'John Brett and the Rossettis', *The Journal of Pre-Raphaelite Studies*, vol. v, no. ii, May 1985, pp. 105-10

Hickox 1996: Mike Hickox, 'John Brett's Portraits', *Review of the Pre-Raphaelite Society*, vol. ix, no. i, 1996, pp. 13-19

Hickox 1998: Mike Hickox, 'John Brett's Lady with a Dove', *Review of the Pre-Raphaelite Society*, vol. vi, no. i, Spring 1998, pp. 12-16

Hudson 1972: Derek Hudson, *Munby: Man of Two Worlds. The Life and Diaries of Arthur J. Munby 1828-1910*, London, 1972

JBD: 'John Brett, Diary 1851-61', typescript, edited by Charles Brett (original in Brett family papers)

Linder 1966: Leslie Linder, ed., *The Journal of Beatrix Potter 1881 - 1897*, London, 1966

Lloyd and Sloan 2008: Stephen Lloyd, Kim Sloan, *The Intimate Portrait: Drawings, Miniatures and Pastels from Ramsay to Lawrence*, exhibition catalogue, National Galleries of Scotland, Edinburgh, the British Museum, London, 2008

Marine Painters 1894: *Loan Collection of Paintings in Oil and Watercolours by Living British Marine Painters*, exhibition catalogue, City of Birmingham Museum and Art Gallery, 1894

Marsh 1985: Jan Marsh, *Pre-Raphaelite Sisterhood*, London, 1985

Marsh 1994: Jan Marsh, *Christina Rossetti: A Literary Biography*, London, 1994

Munby MS: 'Diary of Arthur J. Munby', manuscript, courtesy of the Master and Fellows of Trinity College, Cambridge

Payne 2010: Christiana Payne, *John Brett, Pre-Raphaelite Landscape Painter*, New Haven and London, 2010

Penzance 2006: Charles Brett, Michael Hickox, Christiana Payne, *John Brett: A Pre-Raphaelite in Cornwall*, exhibition catalogue, Penlee House Gallery & Museum, Penzance

Pettigrew 1981: John Pettigrew, ed., *Robert Browning: The Poems*, New Haven and London, 1981

RBSA: Royal Birmingham Society of Artists

Roberts and Wildman 1997: Leonard Roberts, Stephen Wildman, *Arthur Hughes: His Life and Works*, Woodbridge, 1997

Rossetti 1906: William Michael Rossetti, *Some Reminiscences*, New York and London, 1906

Sketchbook: 'John Brett's sketchbooks', National Maritime Museum, Greenwich, London

SL: 'Studio Log kept by John Brett A.R.A. at 38 Harley Street, London', 1887-94, and 'Studio Log, Daisyfield, Putney 1894. Containing Records of Pictorial Transactions, by John Brett A.R.A.' (originals in Brett family papers)

Staley 1973: Allen Staley, *The Pre-Raphaelite Landscape*, Oxford, 1973

Staley and Newall 2004: Allen Staley, Christopher Newall, *Pre-Raphaelite Vision: Truth to Nature*, exhibition catalogue, Tate Britain, 2004

Transactions 1891: John Brett, 'Education in Art', *Transactions of the National Association for the Advancement of Art and its Application to Industry*, London, 1891

Wildman 1995: Stephen Wildman, Jan Marsh, John Christian, *Visions of Love and Life: Pre-Raphaelite Art from the Birmingham Collection, England*, exhibition catalogue, Art Services International, 1995

List of Lenders

Public Institutions

The Ashmolean Museum, Oxford

Birmingham Museums & Art Gallery

The Trustees of the British Museum, London

Andrew Brownsword Arts Foundation

The Syndics of the Fitzwilliam Museum, Cambridge

The Mistress and Fellows of Girton College, Cambridge

National Maritime Museum, Greenwich, London

National Portrait Gallery, London

Tate, London

Private Lenders

Mr and Mrs Balaam

Charles Brett

Martin Brett

Valerie Jill Brett

Helen Brett-Warburton

Richard De Zoysa

Christopher Gridley

Katharine Macdonald

Lord Margadale of Islay

Jenny Newall

Gillian Watson

Peter Watson

Charles Young

Photographic Credits

nos. 1, 2, 5, 6, 7, 8, 10, 11, 12, 14, 15, 17, 19, 21, 23, 24, 25, 26, 27, 28, 29, 30, 32, 34, 43	Private collections/photos: Roy Fox
no. 3	© Tate, London 2010
no. 4	The Mistress and Fellows of Girton College, Cambridge/ photo: Roy Fox
nos. 9, 31	© The Trustees of the British Museum
no. 13	© National Portrait Gallery, London
no. 16	Private collection/Bridgeman Art Library
nos. 18, 20	© Ashmolean Museum, University of Oxford
no. 22	© The Fitzwilliam Museum, University of Cambridge
no. 33	Lord Margadale of Islay/photo: Roy Fox
nos. 35, 36, 37	© National Maritime Museum, Greenwich, London
no. 38	Andrew Brownsword Arts Foundation/photo: The Barber Institute of Fine Arts, University of Birmingham
no. 39	Private collection/photo: National Museum of Wales, Cardiff
nos. 40, 41	Birmingham Museums & Art Gallery
no. 42	The Barber Institute of Fine Arts, University of Birmingham/Bridgeman Art Library
fig. 1	National Museums Liverpool, The Walker/Bridgeman Art Library
figs. 2, 8, 16	Private collections/Bridgeman Art Library
fig. 3	© The Fitzwilliam Museum, University of Cambridge
fig. 4	© Ashmolean Museum, University of Oxford
figs. 5, 7, 25	Private collection/photos: Roy Fox
fig. 6	© Tate, London 2010
figs. 9, 10	Private collection/photo: Rupert Maas
figs. 11, 12, 13, 14, 17, 23, 28, 29, 30	Private collections
fig. 15	RBSA/photo: Luke Unsworth
figs. 18, 19, 22	Birmingham Museums & Art Gallery
fig. 20	Private collection/photo: courtesy of Sotheby's
fig. 21	National Museum of Wales, Cardiff
fig. 24	Sunderland Museum & Winter Gardens, Tyne & Wear Archive & Museums
fig. 26	Aberdeen Art Gallery and Museum
figs. 27, 31	Lord Margadale of Islay/photos: Roy Fox